GREEN GOLD
Bananas and Dependency
in the Eastern Caribbean

Latin America
Bureau

First published in Great Britain in 1987 by
Latin America Bureau (Research and Action) Limited
1 Amwell Street
London EC1R 1UL

Copyright (c) Latin America Bureau (Research and Action) Limited 1987

Published with the assistance of WOW Campaigns Ltd

British Library Cataloguing in Publication Data

Thomson, Robert
    Green gold: bananas and dependency in
    the Eastern Caribbean.
    1. Banana trade — Caribbean area
    I. Title
    338.1'74772'091821   HD9259.B2

ISBN 0-906156-36-X
ISBN 0-906156-26-2 Pbk

Written by Robert Thomson with additional material by George Brizan,
David Demacque, James Ferguson, P I Gomes, Steve Nathan, Jenny Pearce
and Philip Wolmuth

Cover design by Jan Brown, photograph by Philip Wolmuth
Map by Michael Green (c) Latin America Bureau
Trade distribution by Third World Publications, 151 Stratford Road,
Birmingham B11 1RD
Distributed in USA and Canada by Monthly Review Foundation, New
York
Typeset, printed and bound by Russell Press, Nottingham

Contents

The Song of the Banana Man

Touris, white man, wipin his face,
Met me in Golden Grove market place.
He looked at m'ol' clothes brown wid stain,
An soaked right through wid de Portlan rain,
He cas his eye, turned up his nose,
He says, 'You're a beggar man, I suppose?'
He says, 'Boy, get some occupation,
Be of some value to your nation.'

I said, 'By God and dis big right han,
You mus recognise a banana man.'

'Up in de hills, where de streams are cool,
An mullet and janga swim in de pool,
I have ten acres of mountain side,
And a dainty-foot donkey dat I ride,
Four Gros Michel, an four Lacatan,
Some coconut trees, and some hills of yam,
An I pasture on dat very same lan
Five she-goats an big black ram.

Dat, by God and dis big right hand,
Is de property of the banana man.

'I leave m'yard early-morning time
And set m'foot to de mountain climb,
I ben m'back to de hot-sun toil,
An m'cutlass rings on de stony soil,
Ploughin and weedin, diggin and plantin
Till Massa sun drop back o John Crow mountain,
Den home again in cool evenin time,
Perhaps whistling dis likkle rhyme,

(Sung) Praise God and m'big right han,
I will live an die a banana man.'

'Banana day is my special day
I cut my stems an I'm on m'way,
Load up de donkey, leave de lan,
Head down de hill to banana stan,
When de truck comes roun I take a ride
All de way down to de harbour side —
Dat is de night, when you, touris man,
Would change your place wid a banana man.

Yes, by God, and m'big right han,
I will live an die a banana man.

De bay is calm, and de moon is bright
De hills look black for de sky is light,
Down at de dock is an English ship,
Restin after her ocean trip,
While on de pier is a monstrous hustle,
Tallymen, carriers, all in a bustle,
Wid stems on deir heads in a a long black snake
Some singin de songs dat banana men make,

Like (sung) Praise God and m'big right han
I will live an die a banana man.'

'Den de payment comes, an we have some fun,
Me, Zekiel, Breda and Duppy Son.
Down at de bar near United wharf,
We knock back a white rum, bus a laugh,
Fill de empty bag for further toil
Wid saltfish, breadfruit, coconut oil.
Den head back home to m'yard to sleep,
A proper sleep dat is long and deep.

Yes, by God, and m'big right han
I will live an die a banana man.

So when you see dese old clothes brown wid stain,
An soaked right through wid de Portlan rain,
Don't cas your eye nor turn your nose,
Don't judge a man by his patchy clothes,
I'm a strong man, a proud man, an I'm free
Free as dese mountains, free as dis sea,
I know myself, an I know my ways,
An will say wid pride to de end o my days.

(sung) Praise God an m'big right han
I will live an die a banana man.'

Evan Jones

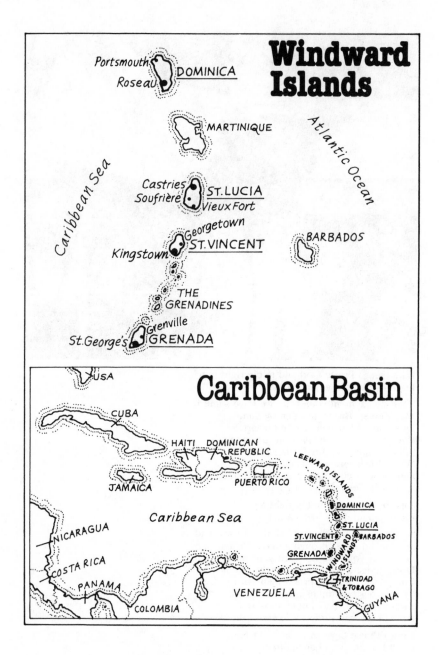

Windward Islands

Portsmouth
Roseau
DOMINICA

MARTINIQUE

Atlantic Ocean

Caribbean Sea

Castries
Soufrière
ST. LUCIA
Vieux Fort

Georgetown
Kingstown
ST. VINCENT

BARBADOS

THE
GRENADINES

Grenville
St. George's
GRENADA

Caribbean Basin

USA

CUBA

HAITI
DOMINICAN
REPUBLIC

JAMAICA

PUERTO RICO

LEEWARD ISLANDS

DOMINICA

ST. LUCIA

ST. VINCENT
BARBADOS

GRENADA
WINDWARD ISLANDS

Caribbean Sea

NICARAGUA

COSTA RICA

PANAMA

VENEZUELA

TRINIDAD
& TOBAGO

COLOMBIA

GUYANA

Statistical profile

	Dominica	Grenada	St Lucia	St Vincent
Population (mid 1983)	81,300	108,800	126,600	113,900
Area (square km)	750	345	616	388
Health — life expectancy (yrs)	58	63	69	67
Education — literacy (%)	80	98	80	80
Unemployment (official figures %)	13	30	14.5	40
Economy				
GDP 1983 (US$ million)	78.5	115.9	138.8	90.4
per capita GDP 1983 (US$)	966	1,065	1,096	794
GDP by sector 1981-83 (%)				
Agriculture	29.9	21.3	13.9	15.5
Manufacturing	7.8	2.6	9.7	11.0
Tourism	1.2	4.4	7.6	2.3
Government	3.6	21.1	22.1	18.9
Other	57.5	50.6	46.7	63.3
External public debt (1983 US$ million)	33.2	48.4	42.3	20.9
Trade balance (1984 US$ million)	−16.4	−32.1	−32.4	−20.8
Bananas				
Working population employed in agriculture (%)	40.0	41.2	39.5	16.8
Bananas as % of total exports (1984)	43.1	16.7	46.8	23.2
Cocoa	—	33.7	—	—
Nutmeg	—	15.6	—	—
Volume of exports (1986 tonnes)	49,100	8,000	107,700	38,000

Currency US$1.00=EC$2.70 (May 1987)

Sources: Economist Intelligence Unit, 1985, 1987. WINBAN, 1987.
Caribbean Insight.

Introduction

Enslavement

On the lower eastern angle of the Caribbean archipelago lie the four Windward Islands of Dominica, Grenada, St Lucia and St Vincent and the Grenadines. In distinction to the Greater Antilles of Cuba, Haiti and the Dominican Republic, Puerto Rico and Jamaica, they have been included among what are known as the Lesser Antilles from the 15th century onwards. Today, with the three northerly islands of Antigua-Barbuda, Montserrat and St Kitts-Nevis, they constitute the Organisation of Eastern Caribbean States (OECS).

From the earliest arrival of European powers in the Caribbean, these four islands were the object of fierce inter-colonial rivalry. In the course of the 17th and 18th centuries they were to change hands regularly between Britain and France, as the two European nations fought for economic and strategic control within the region. It was finally Britain which successfully claimed the four islands as colonies; Dominica, Grenada and St Vincent came under British rule in 1763, and St Lucia in 1814. Yet French influence remains strong even today, most notably in place names and in the French patois which is widely spoken in St Lucia.

The indigenous inhabitants of the Windward Islands, the Caribs, who had long resisted colonisation, were eventually exterminated or deported to the Central American mainland, while British and French colonists attempted to insert the islands into the prevailing regional model of sugar production. Here, they encountered significant problems, since the colonies were not only too small for large-scale plantation production, but were also geographically unsuitable with their mountainous, and sometimes volcanic, terrain. In comparison with other islands such as Barbados and Trinidad, the Windward territories were by no means ideal for sugar growing. Nevertheless, such was the importance attached to sugar that the islands were almost exclusively given over to production of this one crop.

The plantations were generally small in size and output, each containing relatively few slaves. When claims for compensation were filed by the Windward planters with the abolition of slavery in 1833,

1

there was reckoned to be an average of only fifteen slaves on each plantation. As elsewhere in the Caribbean, abolition created an immediate shortage of labour in the sugar plantations, and indentured workers, mostly from India, were brought to Grenada, St Lucia and St Vincent. At the same time, large numbers of former slaves abandoned the plantations and either rented or squatted on small patches of land. Consequently an unequal pattern of land distribution developed, in which small farmers and peasants occupied smallholdings, while the colonial plantocracy maintained control of the larger estates. Many peasants could not subsist on their smallholdings alone, as these tended to be situated on the most marginal and least fertile land; they were therefore forced also to work on the plantations. Sharecropping and various quasi-feudal arrangements evolved too; many of these survive until the present day.

From sugar to bananas

As sugar declined as an export at the end of the 19th century — due partly to the success of mechanised production in Cuba and partly to European beet growing — the Windward Islands and their colonial plantocracies faced an escalating economic crisis. The response of the colonial authorities was to recommend a programme of land settlement, whereby plantation workers could obtain greater access to smallholdings. This recommendation, forcefully expressed by the British West Indian Royal Commission of 1897, was rejected by the planters, whose archaic methods and obstinate attachment to sugar production ruled out significant redistribution of land. A large proportion of the sugar estates remained idle — the price of sugar had dropped disastrously — yet the plantocracy was unwilling to encourage any changes which might threaten its own effective monopoly of land ownership. The peasantry was accordingly restricted to renting and leasehold tenure, while freehold ownership was effectively prohibited.

Slowly, however, the dominance of sugar began to weaken as other crops were produced for export from the Windward Islands. These other crops — such as arrowroot, cocoa, nutmeg, limes and bananas — were more suited to the islands' smaller estates and required less capital investment from the owners who could not compete with the large, capital intensive operations in other colonies. As a result, smallholders gained a firmer foothold in the islands and partially reduced their dependency upon the plantocracy, although the latter kept control of the best available land. Some measure of agricultural diversification, partly for local consumption but mostly for export, was

2

therefore forced upon the recalcitrant planter class in the first decades of the 20th century.

Bananas eventually superceded sugar completely as the major export of the Windward Islands, reinforcing the domination of the large planters. The first stage in this process occurred in 1925 when the Swift Banana Company (a subsidiary of the US company United Fruit) acquired land for banana production in St Lucia. The venture was short-lived however, since Panama disease destroyed the prevalent variety of banana and the Company was liquidated in 1927. By 1933 a second attempt to establish a banana industry was made by another subsidiary of United Fruit, the Canadian Buying Company. Again, disease undermined production and this, together with the disruption to trade caused by World War II, led to the destruction of the industry by 1941.

These first tentative experiments in banana production took place against a backcloth of mounting social unrest in the British Caribbean. Poverty and malnutrition were widespread throughout the region. In the underdeveloped Windward Islands, where wages were even lower than in Jamaica or Trinidad-Tobago, social conditions were especially harsh for the majority of people. A wave of strikes and riots in the 1930s reflected the growth of trade union militancy and political frustration. In all, 47 people died, 400 were injured and canefields and estate buildings were burned in a series of disturbances throughout the region. In some areas martial law was declared and British troops were brought in to restore order. The disturbances were mainly centred in the larger colonies of Jamaica, Trinidad-Tobago and British Guiana, yet some rioting also occurred in St Vincent in 1935.

Such unrest prompted concern from the British colonial authorities, and a number of official commissions were sent to the region to report on conditions and to propose remedies. Of these, the most influential was the West India Royal Commission of 1939, led by Lord Moyne, which published its full recommendations in 1945. Noting the profoundly unequal distribution of land between plantations and peasants, the Commission wrote of the latter that: 'their situation offers an admirable opportunity for social reform.' In effect, the Moyne Commission reiterated the recommendations of the 1897 report, and urged increased land settlement and a programme of agricultural diversification and self-sufficiency.

Plans to reform land distribution proposed in London, ran counter to the entrenched interests of the islands' reactionary plantocracy. This land-owning class was comprised of the remnants of the traditional, absentee sugar planters and of a local bourgeoisie which combined estate ownership with business, principally trading interests. It continued to exert a near monopoly over the islands' most

3

fertile and accessible land, hence pushing the peasantry into the least economically viable areas. Whether as smallholders or landless estate workers, the peasantry was still largely dependent upon the plantation system. The gulf between large and small landowners increased, moreover, as the more successful plantations expanded by buying up less profitable estates.

A new wave of militancy shook the region and culminated in the general strike of 1951 in Grenada, led by Eric Gairy. The strike demonstrated the strength of a unionised agricultural workforce and posed a challenge to the plantocracy and the colonial authorities. After a state of emergency had been declared and British naval units had been summoned, the strike was ended, but only after many of the strikers' demands had been met. Gairy himself was to use the support of Grenada's workers to obtain political power and then opportunistically to seek accommodation with the colonial authorities. Yet, nevertheless the renewed unrest in the Windward Islands presented further problems for London and the local landowners.

Bananas and communism

New tactics clearly had to be sought for the restoration of social stability in the region. The British government had to neutralise discontent in the islands without endangering its own economic and strategic interests. One possible means of achieving this aim was to encourage the development of an alternative agricultural system which would replace dependence upon the traditional export cash crop of sugar. In this context, bananas seemed to offer a viable alternative and promised certain distinct advantages.

Banana production required minimal capital outlay and in many ways was ideally suited to maintaining the status quo on the islands. Bananas could be grown on large estates or on tiny hillside plots. They could be intercropped with staple food crops. They would fruit throughout the year — unlike sugar or other crops which produce one or two harvests a year — and they would provide a regular, although small, income. This was crucial for the majority of Windward Island farmers who owned plots of five acres or less, living a hand-to-mouth existence with little or no savings to tide them over between harvests.

The West India Committee, a coalition of colonial and regional business interests including Elders and Fyffes Ltd, saw banana production as a plausible vehicle for social stabilisation through the promotion of small-scale (as well as large-scale) private enterprise. A report in the Committee circular of December 1955 entitled, 'bananas

4

and communism', neatly encapsulated the political dimension of such a shift in agricultural production:

> A brochure recently issued to shareholders by the United Fruit Company gives a glimpse of the way in which the operations of the company demonstrate the contribution which private enterprise can make to the cultural and economic development of a country, and also, through a carefully planned programme of advertising, public relations and day-to-day human relations, can help to carry the message of democracy to the people, 'who will then (as they recently did in Guatemala) rise in their wrath and repel any Communist threat to their liberties'. Good deeds, state the company, are basic, but they also need to be merchandised, and the brochure gives some particulars of the tactics employed to publicise widely and constantly the social and economic benefits that accrue under the democratic free enterprise system.

Sections of the colonial lobby, therefore, perceived the advantages of a banana industry in the Windward Islands as both economic and political. By encouraging the growth of the industry, it was suggested, a collaborative class of petty capitalists could be created which would have no stake in future social unrest. This view, however, was not entirely shared by other sections within the colonial administration. The West India Royal Commission of 1945 had warned of the dangers of over-specialisation in bananas, citing the risks of Panama disease and soil erosion. It had concluded:

> Every government in these Colonies should show caution in dealing with matters affecting banana growing. There is in all the Colonies and among all classes of cultivator a desire to grow bananas because of the regular cash income they ensure.

In the event, commercial considerations outweighed such official misgivings. The way was by now open for a British company — Geest — to exploit the possibilities of a banana industry in the Windward Islands.

Towards independence

British projects to stabilise the region were a reflection of the slow process of colonial disengagement. A gradual liberalisation of the Crown Colony system after World War I, allowing for increased local representation in government, was followed by the Labour administration's granting of universal adult suffrage in 1950 and 1961. Subsequent elections in the Windward Islands brought to power labour-based parties in all four colonies. The islands were then incorporated into the controversial and abortive West Indies Federation which lasted only four years from its foundation in 1958.

There followed the phase of Associated Statehood, in which the Windward Islands were self-governing, but dependent upon Britain for defence and foreign policy.

During this period from 1966 to full independence in the 1970s, the Windward Islands followed the 'Westminster model' of parliamentary democracy. The ruling political parties which had emerged in the 1950s remained dominant and their leaderships perennial. These leading political personalities were either populists from trade union backgrounds, as was the case with Gairy in Grenada and Patrick John in Dominica, or were conservative, middle class professionals, such as John Compton in St Lucia and Milton Cato in St Vincent. The four premiers, all claiming to represent some form of labourism, enjoyed long periods in office in the course of the 1960s and 1970s and followed broadly similar political programmes.

In Gordon K Lewis's phrase, the Windward Islands' governments formulated 'a combination of borrowed Labour Party rhetoric and domestic social paternalism'. Their principal objective was to attract foreign investment and contain domestic political radicalism. A growing dependency upon US capital was accompanied by anti-union legislation as the islands' governments attempted to follow the Puerto Rican model of 'industrialisation by invitation'. Industrial parks were constructed, tax holidays and other incentives were offered to potential investors, and trade union activity was repressed. In St Lucia and St Vincent in particular, manufacturing became an important sector of the economy; over 70 foreign operations were established in St Lucia in the course of the 1970s. Despite considerable foreign investment however, unemployment remained high and wages low.

Corruption became an intrinsic feature of the region during the period preceding independence. The regimes of Eric Gairy and Patrick John were especially associated with illegal practices. In Dominica, for instance, John agreed a secret deal whereby the government was to lease a large tract of land to a firm which hoped to construct a free port or trans-shipment terminal to 'launder' the sale of petroleum to South Africa. The public outcry contributed to John's resignation in 1979. His successor, Oliver Seraphine, promptly signed a similar deal with the Los Angeles based Intercontinental Development and Management Company, which was intended to give the company tax-free control of Dominica's tourist industry, banking interests and other industries. This too was stopped by the electoral defeat of Seraphine in 1980.

These excesses were symptomatic of a more generalised corruption which surrounded the structure and function of the state in the small islands. The introduction of universal suffrage in the 1950s had eroded the political monopoly of the plantocracy and had assisted the rise of an urban, professional middle class in its place. This class was able to win political office and develop an economic base for itself by using the power of the state. Monopoly import privileges, tax concessions, government contracts, patronage, land expropriations and other legal and illegal actions allowed it to control the expanding urban sectors of construction, tourism and small manufacturing. Party officials and loyalists found their rewards under this system.

Winds of change

The advent of full independence brought little change in St Lucia and St Vincent. In St Lucia, which became independent in 1979, John Compton's United Workers Party returned to power in 1982 after a factional split within the opposition St Lucia Labour Party. Campaigning on the slogan 'Christians ever, Communists never', Compton pledged to pursue pro-US policies. Five years after independence in St Vincent, Milton Cato's St Vincent Labour Party was defeated in 1984 by James Mitchell's New Democratic Party. The new government promised no significant change in economic direction.

The collapse of the Labour Party of Dominica however, transformed the political situation in the Windward Islands' least developed country. Two years after independence in 1978, the landslide electoral victory of Eugenia Charles and the Dominica Freedom Party signalled a major shift to the right. Charles, a lawyer from a wealthy land-owning family, was an enthusiastic supporter of the Reagan administration and of US regional interests. In the wake of an abortive coup attempt, the Dominican government passed a draconian Anti-Terrorism Act in 1980 and declared a state of emergency the following year. Political repression was combined with economic liberalism, which included an agreement with the IMF and a programme to privatise the most important sectors of the banana industry (see Dominica case study).

The principal political development within the region occurred in Grenada, which became independent in 1974. On 13 March 1979 a popular coup led by the New Jewel Movement, ousted Eric Gairy's regime. Under Gairy, Grenada had experienced years of corruption, incompetence and repression. The island's largest estates and best land were controlled by Gairy and his supporters, while the majority of farmers were confined to tiny and economically unviable smallholdings. Agricultural reform was an immediate priority for the People's Revolutionary Government (PRG). Gairy's estates and much idle land were brought under government control, and state

7

intervention in agriculture provided important improvements within the island's infrastructure which had previously been neglected. A general policy of diversification and food production for local consumption served to reduce Grenada's dependence upon traditional export markets and expensive food imports.

The achievements of the PRG were considerable in the fields of health, housing and education. Grenada's 'non-capitalist' development programme, however, together with its political ties with Cuba, earned the hostility of the US. After a protracted period of economic destabilisation, the US finally capitalised upon the internal disintegration of the PRG and overthrew the revolution through a military invasion of the island in October 1983 (see Grenada case study). Since the invasion, Grenada has returned to a pro-US economic stance under the government of Herbert Blaize and is increasingly dominated by the United States Agency for Economic Development (USAID). The return of Gairy to Grenadian politics also remains a possibility.

'Persistent poverty'

The Windward Islands remain underdeveloped, impoverished and subject to a number of internal and external pressures. Land distribution is still highly unbalanced, as a high proportion of small farmers account for a low share in land ownership (see table). Because banana production is a vital cash earner, other forms of agriculture are given less priority. There is consequently a shortage of basic foodstuffs and significant dependence upon food imports. In 1982, food accounted for 23.4 per cent of Dominica's imports, 27.5 per cent of Grenada's, 21.1 per cent of St Lucia's and 29.2 per cent of St

Land distribution in the Windward Islands (1982)				
	Dominica	St Lucia	St Vincent	Grenada
Acres of bananas	13,000	12,000	6,500	3,500
Number of growers	5,095	6,323	4,894	1,913
% under 1 acre	70	69	61	33
% 1-5 acres	25	23	31	40
% over 5 acres	5	8	8	27

Source: Food and Agricultural Organisation, The World Banana Economy 1970-1984. FAO Economic and Social Development Paper 57, Rome, 1986.

Vincent's. Malnutrition remains a widespread problem.

Besides disease and soil erosion, the local farmers also face the danger of frequent and destructive hurricanes (see box, p.10). Due to deprivation in the countryside, growing numbers of people have moved into urban areas, hoping to find work in the offshore assembly plants. Both in the cities and rural communities, unemployment, particularly among youth, is extremely high and shows little sign of improving (see table).

Windward Islands youth unemployment rates 1980-82
(by age group)

Country	Unemployment rate %	
	15-19 yrs	20-24 yrs
Dominica	55.7	23.8
Grenada	55.8	26.4
St Lucia	52.5	21.8
St Vincent	58.2	24.2

Source: Central Statistical Office, *Vital Statistics Bulletin*. vol 1, no 1, Port of Spain, Trinidad and Tobago, 1986.

Unemployment has in turn led to emigration from the islands as people are forced to look for work in the region and beyond. In the course of the 1970s, it is estimated that some 70,000 people left the Windward Islands as legal or illegal emigrants.

The four Windward Islands are 'beneficiaries' of the Caribbean Basin Initiative, a package of bilateral aid, duty-free concessions to Caribbean countries, and investment inducements to US businesses which operate in the region. Under the terms of the CBI, the Windward Islands have received varying amounts of economic aid from the Reagan administration. At the same time, US companies have set up offshore plants in the islands, taking advantage of tax concessions and cheap labour. In St Lucia and St Vincent in particular, electronic components and garments form an important part of the manufacturing sector. Tourism too, is another source of revenue. All four islands are increasingly dependent upon this 'enclave' industry and upon an influx of largely North American visitors.

US influence is most directly felt however, in the growing militarisation of the Eastern Caribbean. Between 1950 and 1980 the region received no US military aid. Yet between 1980 and 1984 the governments of the islands received at least US$10.5 million in direct military aid. The projected role of an Eastern Caribbean defence force could be foreseen in October 1983, when a token regional security force was sent to Grenada with US troops. Critics of US regional policy, including James Mitchell and the late Errol Barrow (formerly Prime Minister of Barbados), condemned the military build-up as a threat to the islands' sovereignty. 'What use do we have', asked Barrow, 'for a bunch of fellows dressed in fatigues, carrying rifles and shouting 'Hup, two, three, four' all day long?'

A recent boom in banana production has created a substantial influx

---

Hurricanes

Hurricanes are a permanent feature of life in the region. A letter sent on 1 November 1780 by William Mathew Burt, British Governor of the Leeward Islands, to Lord George Germain describes the effect of a single hurricane:

> It is with infinite concern that I have received the following account of the truly severe hurricane which happened in the middle of last month amongst the southern islands... At St Lucia, all the barracks and huts for his majesty's troops, and other buildings were blown down... Every building in St Vincent, we are told, was blown down and the town destroyed...The houses and everything in Grenada, I hear, are levelled with the ground.

More recently, hurricanes David in August 1979 and Allen in 1980 wreaked havoc with the islands' banana industries. In St Lucia, hurricane Allen destroyed 100 per cent of the banana crop, causing an estimated EC$93 million of damage. Damage in St Vincent, which lost 95 per cent of its crop, was put at EC$11 million, while Grenada lost 40 per cent of its crop, worth EC$6 million.

Post-hurricane reconstruction grants were made by the United States Agency for International Development (USAID). Dominica received US$1.5 million, St Vincent US$0.8 million and St Lucia US$0.47 million. Grenada, which was then under the People's Revolutionary Government, received nothing.

---

of export earnings into the Windward Islands, most notably in St Lucia, and has resulted in large increases in income for farmers. This situation is due to a dramatic increase in production, largely as a result of the introduction of the field packing system (see chapter 3). The consequences of the boom are to be seen in a rapid expansion of private consumption, as farmers have more cash to spend on goods, most of which are imported. Cars, televisions and other consumer durables have poured into the islands. The boom has principally occurred within the private sector. In St Lucia which has no income tax in agriculture, the government receives no extra revenue for essential public spending and development.

The outlook for the industry is one of continuing expansion. This may lead to further short-term increases in export earnings, but may also result in over-production and therefore lower average prices for producers, in the longer term. Furthermore, the industry remains particularly vulnerable to climatic risks. Production in 1986 benefited from optimum levels of rainfall and relatively little wind damage. There can be no guarantee that these conditions will continue and that the industry will not return to the catastrophic situation of 1980.

Generally, the future of the Windward Islands remains uncertain. While farmers rush to plant bananas in response to the present boom, there are no guarantees of sustained growth. In the meantime, much ecological damage is being done by planting bananas on unsuitable terrain. The present boom is merely postponing the search for a more balanced and equitable development.

It seems particularly short-sighted that the governments of the region are not taking advantage of the increase in incomes by channelling resources through taxation into public spending. Nor do there appear to be any serious regional attempts to develop the islands' economic potential. Proposals put forward in 1987 for greater political integration between the seven OECS territories could produce a more unified regional market and alleviate some of the problems specific to the Caribbean 'micro-states', though many doubt that they could ever become a reality. Such administrative and political reforms would in any case be unlikely to change the structure of the banana industry and the dependency associated with it in any significant way.

Within this structure of dependency the small farmers of the Windward Islands are exceptionally atomised and economically weak. They have learned to adapt to the prevailing system, and are able to capitalise upon short-term conditions of expansion and increased opportunities for cash income. The ethos of individualism encouraged by the British Foreign Office in the 1950s, has taken root, with the result that there is little tradition of collective and cooperative activity. In this sense, their lives are all the more determined by a high-risk occupation and by decisions taken in London, in which they have little or no say. Bananas, the region's principal economic mainstay, provide a vital, if highly unpredictable, cash income. If 'green gold' can generate short-term, relative affluence for the small farmer and real wealth for the large producer, it nevertheless perpetuates an economy which is ultimately fragile and beyond the control of the great majority.

Large scale production in La Ceiba, Honduras

Jenny Matthews

1 The international banana market

The Windward Islands play a very small role in the global banana trade, though banana exports are vital to the livelihoods of their inhabitants. This chapter puts the islands' banana industry in its international context.

Although many of the problems facing the islands are very different in character to those of the larger Latin American producers, they share those of export dependence, foreign exchange shortages and poor living standards. Also in common is their reliance on

---

Whose gold?

A major study recently completed by the UNCTAD secretariat suggests that for world banana trade taken as a whole, only 11.5 per cent of the total value of bananas generated at the retail level accrues as retained value to the national economies which export them. The remaining 88.5 per cent accrues to foreign enterprises originating in the importing countries, and owned and operated by importing country citizens. These include the multinational companies, other trading concerns, independent importers, ripeners, wholesalers and retailers. Although the data base underlying this calculation is incomplete and, in some cases, inaccurate, there is a reasonable degree of certainty that the broad magnitudes are correct. Out of a total retail value of US$2,114 million generated in 1971, the producing countries received approximately US$245 million in retained value.

Conventional rationalities would attach little importance to this distribution of gains. The argument would run that provided the market worked competitively and efficiently so that bananas were produced at least cost, and there was no exercise of monopoly wither to depress returns to producers or overcharge consumers, then there would be no cause for alarm. But development is an historical process, not a static equilibrium: it involves amongst other factors the need to generate a surplus for re-investment, the need to acquire managerial and technical expertise in the population, the need to establish activities with a more diversely derived, and greater value-added than the mere production of an unprocessed agricultural commodity. The main force of the

▶

---

multinational corporations who control the profitable marketing and
distribution side of the banana industry, as well as other aspects of it.
While Geest is hardly comparable to the infamous 'big three'
companies who have traditionally dominated the industry in Latin
America, its power, resources and ability to diversify and innovate,
contrast greatly with the situation of the poor nations in which it
operates.

The producers

In 1983 world banana exports, amounting to just over six million
tonnes, were worth US$1.9 billion. The vast bulk (85 per cent) were
produced in the third world and consumed in the developed capitalist
economies (see tables). Most banana exporting countries are poor and
have rapidly growing populations. With the exception of Panama,
Costa Rica and the Caribbean islands of Jamaica, Martinique and

World consumption of bananas (1982)			
Region	Major suppliers	Volume ('000 tonnes)	Share (%) Imports / per capita
North America		(2594.4)	(37.96) —
United States	Ecuador, Costa Rica, Honduras	2325.0	34.02 10.0
Canada	Ecuador, Colombia, Honduras	269.4	3.94 10.9
European Economic Community		(1857.7)	(27.18) —
West Germany	Panama, Costa Rica, Honduras	503.0	7.36 8.2
France	Martinique, Guadeloupe	466.8	6.83 8.6
United Kingdom	WINBAN, Colombia, Suriname	322.0	4.71 5.7
Italy	Colombia, Costa Rica, Somalia	330.0	4.83 5.8
Others		235.9	3.45 —

Other Western Europe		(751.6)	(11.00)	—
Spain	Canary Islands	415.0	6.07	11.0
Austria	Costa Rica, Panama, Honduras	77.3	1.13	10.3
Sweden	Panama, Costa Rica, Honduras	72.3	1.06	8.7
Switzerland	Panama, Costa Rica, Honduras	58.4	0.85	9.1
Finland	Costa Rica, Ecuador	45.0	0.66	8.5
Others		83.6	1.22	—
Eastern Europe, USSR		(151.9)	(2.22)	—
East Germany	Ecuador, Colombia	60.0	0.88	3.6
USSR	Ecuador	46.0	0.67	0.2
Czechoslovakia	Colombia, Costa Rica, Ecuador	26.0	0.38	1.7
Hungary	Colombia, Ecuador	14.8	0.22	1.4
Bulgaria		5.1	0.07	0.6
Sub total — developed countries		6149.5	89.98	—
Asia		(1094.3)	(16.01)	—
Japan	Phillipines, China	757.9	11.09	6.4
New Zealand		36.0	0.53	11.4
Saudi Arabia	Phillipines, Guatemala, Ecuador	120.0	1.76	12.4
Kuwait		35.0	0.51	22.9
Hong Kong		30.0	0.44	5.6
China		20.0	0.29	—
Others		95.4	1.40	—
Africa		(84.8)	(1.24)	—
Libya		30.0	0.44	9.3
Algeria		18.0	0.26	0.9
Tunisia		14.0	0.20	2.1
Others		22.8	0.33	—
Latin America		(299.8)	(4.39)	—
Argentina	Ecuador, Brazil, Colombia	140.0	2.05	5.1
Chile	Ecuador	87.8	1.28	7.6
El Salvador		37.0	0.54	7.3
Uruguay		35.0	0.51	11.8
Sub total — developing countries		685.0	10.02	—
World Totals		6834.5	100.00	—

Source: FAO, World Banana Economy: Statistical Compendium (Economic and Social Development Paper 31), Rome, 1983

15

World banana exports (1982)

Region	Major markets	Volume ('000 tonnes)	Share (%)
UPEB countries		(3476.5)	(49.98)
Colombia	US, Holland, Italy, France	733.0	10.54
Costa Rica	US, W Germany, Italy	919.0	13.21
Dom. Republic	US	14.7	0.21
Guatemala	US, Italy, Canada	380.2	5.47
Honduras	US, W Germany, Holland	820.0	11.79
Nicaragua	US	43.4	0.62
Panama	US, W Germany, Belgium	563.2	8.10
Venezuela		3.0	0.04
Other Latin America		(1371.6)	(19.72)
Ecuador	US, Belgium, Chile, Argentina	1254.3	18.03
Brazil	Argentina, Uruguay	63.0	0.91
Suriname	UK, Italy	37.5	0.54
Belize	US	9.5	0.14
Mexico	US	7.3	0.10
Caribbean		(413.7)	(5.95)
Jamaica	UK	21.9	0.31
WINBAN	UK	112.9	1.62
Dominica	UK	28.5	0.41
St Lucia	UK	47.0	0.68
St Vincent	UK	27.6	0.40
Grenada	UK	9.8	0.14
Guadeloupe	France	122.2	1.76
Martinique	France, Italy	156.7	2.25
Asia		(1047.3)	(15.06)
Phillipines	Japan, Saudi Arabia, Kuwait	900.0	12.94
China		94.0	1.35
Vietnam		8.0	0.12
Others		45.3	0.65
Africa		(194.3)	(2.79)
Cameroun	France, UK	53.0	0.76
Ivory Coast	France, Italy	85.0	1.22
Somalia	Italy	48.3	0.69
Others		8.0	0.12
Oceania		7.0	0.10
Sub total — developing countries		6510.4	93.59
Developed countries		446.0	6.41
Portugal (Madeira)		28.0	0.40
Spain (Canary Islands)		415.0	5.97
Israel		3.0	0.04
World totals		6956.4	100.00

Source: FAO, World Banana Economy: Statistical Compendium, (Economic and Development Paper 31), Rome, 1983.

Guadeloupe, they all have a *per capita* income of less than US$500 per year. This compares with *per capita* incomes of US$10,000 and more in the consuming countries.

Until the early 1970s bananas were by far the most important fresh fruit entering international trade. Since then, oranges have overtaken them in volume and value. But to the developing countries, bananas remain one of the most important exported tropical crops, fifth in value after sugar, coffee, cocoa and rubber.

Over the years the degree of dependence of developing countries on bananas for foreign exchange earnings has changed. Until the early 1970s a number of countries depended on bananas for over half their export earnings. Today, only the Windward Islands remain so dependent, with bananas accounting for as much as 60 per cent of export earnings in the islands as a group. Five other suppliers — Costa Rica, Honduras, Panama, Guadeloupe and Martinique — depend on bananas for 20 per cent or more of their export earnings. For the remaining suppliers, bananas contribute less than 10 per cent of such earnings.

Foreign exchange earnings are only one measure of the importance of bananas to the economies of developing countries. They are often also a major source of employment and income in the rural economy of a country. Banana production is still relatively labour-intensive despite the highly capital-intensive nature of many of the inputs used. In Ecuador, the share of bananas in export earnings fell from over 60 per cent in the early 1960s to under 10 per cent in the 1980s as a result of growing oil exports. But Ecuador is still one of the largest banana exporters in the world and bananas are a major source of employment. In the Windward Islands, bananas employ an estimated average of 30 per cent of the working population.

The markets

There is no single world market for bananas. Historical links between exporting and importing countries have shaped today's banana trade flows so that a number of bilateral preferential trading arrangements exist alongside the open market, which is not subject to government interference.

By far the largest sector of the world banana market is the open market, which accounts for about 63 per cent of world imports. Open markets cover major trade flows from Central and South America to North America and the non-preferential markets of western Europe. This trade is dominated by three multinational companies whose role will be discussed below. Trade from the Philippines and China to

Japan is also under open market conditions and is the second largest flow of trade.

About 17 per cent of world banana imports (the third largest flow of trade) are covered by preferential markets. Preferential access under quota and licensing arrangements to France is given to exports from the French Overseas Departments of Martinique and Guadeloupe, and to the UK from the Commonwealth Caribbean (Jamaica and the Windward Islands). Other associated states of EEC countries in Africa export mainly to the EEC: Cameroun to France; Somalia to Italy; and the Ivory Coast to all the EEC countries. When quotas cannot be filled (as has occurred with the suppliers to the Italian and UK markets) the shortfall is met from open market suppliers.

The fourth largest flow of trade (seven per cent) is domestic trade from the Canary Islands to Spain and from Madeira to Portugal. Another seven per cent is accounted for by minor local trade to nearby markets (such as from Ecuador to Chile, Brazil and Argentina). Sixth are the new markets of Eastern Europe — Yugoslavia and the Soviet Union — and the oil-exporting countries of the Near East and North Africa, accounting for only six per cent of banana imports. In the early to mid-1970s these markets were considered to have substantial growth potential, but since then demand has fallen in all but a few.

The multinationals

The world banana trade is dominated by three US-owned multinational companies. In 1980 the 'big three' — United Brands (formerly United Fruit), Standard Fruit and Del Monte — together controlled 65 per cent of total world banana exports from eight countries. In fact, the share of the multinationals in world banana trade has increased over the past two decades; in 1966 they controlled 47 per cent of trade and in 1972, 54 per cent. They have been the main beneficiaries of the considerable growth in world trade in the 1960s and 1970s, and have been able to sell in preferential markets as a result of supply problems from the Caribbean and African exporters.

The banana industry is characterised, therefore, by what economists call 'oligopoly' ie a handful of firms divide the market between themselves. The big three companies have traditionally exercised enormous power in the countries in which they operate, both politically and economically (see box, p.19). In the first part of this century they came to own vast tracts of prime land in these countries. In 1949 United Fruit owned or leased approximately 3.5 million acres in Cuba, Jamaica, Honduras, Guatemala, Nicaragua, Costa Rica, Panama and Colombia; an amount of land comparable in area to

United Fruit in Honduras

In the 1920s, United Fruit obtained generous franchises in the Tela and Trujillo regions of the Atlantic coast. United Fruit made an agreement with the government to build a railroad from the north coast to the capital in exchange for land and tax exemptions. For each kilometer of railroad built, the companies would receive 550 to 1,100 acres. The mileage laid, however, was little more than what was strictly necessary for the operation of the banana industry, so that it ran through the coastal agricultural lands and never reached the capital of Tegucigalpa.

An example of the company's attitude about doing business in Honduras is a letter written in 1920 by United Fruit's H V Rolston to the company's lawyer in Honduras. He instructed the lawyer to:

> ... obtain rigid contracts of such a nature that no one can compete against us, not even in the distant future, so that any enterprise that could establish and develop itself must be under our control... We must obtain concessions, privileges, franchises, repeal of custom duties, freedom from all public liens, burdens, and all those taxes and obligations which restrict our profits and those of our associates. We must erect a privileged situation in order to impose our commercial philosophy and our economic defense.

The power of *El Pulpo* (the octopus) was challenged for the first time when in 1954 thousands of banana workers won a 69-day strike. Not only did they win this first agricultural strike in Honduran history, but they won official recognition by the state that workers had a formal right to organise. The 1954 strike set the stage for the creation of other peasant and worker unions. The companies reacted in several ways. By 1959, 20,000 banana plantation workers had lost their jobs. Because of mechanisation, the companies were able to increase production while decreasing the number of workers. Between 1950-54, the banana productivity per worker in Honduras was 552 boxes, and twenty years later it was 2,131 boxes per worker. In addition, United Fruit's strategy included infiltration of the union by members associated with the Inter-American Regional Organization of Labor (ORIT) and the American Institute for Free Labor Development (AIFLD), after the founding of AIFLD in 1962. Both organisations are associated with the AFL-CIO in the United States. AIFLD trains union members in programs that stress anti-communism and organising limited wage demands.

A United Fruit employee recalled: 'After the strike, the AFL-CIO, the US Embassy, and ORIT fell on us like a plague, offering us scholarships to 'study in Puerto Rico', and getting us all kinds of favors from our employers... The US consuls overwhelmed us with visas... the greatest interest in these scholarship students is to be found on the north coast land of the banana companies... Not only do these companies

▶

grant their permission for these workers to spend months on leave, but they are favored with the choicest jobs and are placed, very 'democratically' as union leaders, when they return...'

In 1979, progressive workers won back leadership of the union on United Brands' banana plantations and led the first major labor initiative since the 1954 strike. In late 1980, when the union directed a strike in protest of the company's use of harmful pesticides, union leaders received death threats and were fired from their jobs. In this repressive atmosphere, the ORIT-affiliated Confederation of Honduran Workers took over in 1981, making it once again a company union.

Source: Barry, Wood and Preusch, 1982.

In pursuing its ends in Honduras, the United Fruit Company dispensed with the regard for appearances that it showed in other lands. The war minister, Juan Manuel Galvez, the president of Congress, Plutarco Muñoz, and the head of the Supreme Court, were all United Fruit attorneys. There were local commanders on the North Coast who received half their pay from the company. Those not rating a regular salary came in for frequent tips. Before Spruille Braden came to the State Department, journalists who ventured to criticise the banana trust were silenced with bribes, while recalcitrants disappeared into [President] Carías's dungeons.

Source: Krehm, 1984

Switzerland. Large-scale plantation units have traditionally been the dominant pattern of the industry.

Today the 'big three' continue to engage in direct production in Central America, operating plantations as large as 5,000 hectares. But in the post-war period (particularly in the early 1960s following expropriations of United Fruit in Guatemala, Cuba and Ecuador) they cut back on their private holdings and launched associate producer programmes. Under these programmes, the fruit is sold to the multinationals under contract by local banana growers. The programme accelerated somewhat in the 1970s following the formation of the Union of Banana Exporting Countries (UPEB) in 1974 (see below). In 1971 the multinationals produced nearly 70 per cent of the total exports of Costa Rica, Guatemala, Honduras and Panama. This proportion had fallen to 61 per cent by 1984.

In contrast to the large-scale production which is still a major characteristic of the banana industry in Latin America, production in the Windward Islands is dominated by smallholders. Nor do the banana growers of the Windward Islands deal with any of the 'big three'. Since 1954 nearly every banana which leaves the islands has been exported under an exclusive contract with Geest PLC, formerly one of Britain's largest private companies and a public company since November 1986. Geest is the UK's largest importer and distributor of fruit and vegetables. Its imports from the Windward Islands accounted for 62 per cent of the British banana market in 1986, having risen from 39 per cent in 1983. Fyffes, a subsidiary of United Brands, controls a further 30 per cent of the British market.

Fyffes sold 1986

Though not one of the 'big three' (the company accounts for only 1.6 per cent of world banana exports), Geest wields considerable power over the lives and fortunes of the people of the Windward Islands. This takes a rather paternalistic form and is not comparable to the turbulent history of relations between the 'big three' and the countries in which they have traditionally operated.

All banana multinationals have come to share certain operational features, duplicated in many respects by the much smaller company of Geest. The organisational structure shared by the companies is known as 'vertical integration'. In other words, the companies have come to control several phases of banana production and marketing which under free market conditions would be controlled by a number of different companies.

There are five phases involved in getting the bananas to the customer; production, transport, ripening, wholesale and retail distribution. The 'big three' tend to dominate the first four phases most completely. Geest's investments are concentrated in the middle three sectors: transport, ripening and wholesale distribution. Since it is the sole buyer of Windward Island bananas for export, Geest is able to dictate the conditions under which it will accept them. Through its market control, Geest also has considerable influence over production.

Vertical integration gives a multinational company a number of advantages. For example, it can change the price of goods which one division of the same company charges another, since such transactions are internal to one organisation. This system of transfer pricing enables the company, rather than the market, to determine prices. Since many large enterprises operate in great secrecy, it is very difficult even for governments to determine whether the prices set represent a fair value for local production and therefore, whether the company is paying its fair share of national taxes. The company can undervalue goods in countries with high tax rates and increase them in countries with lower rates.

It is clear that 'vertical integration' gives the banana companies considerable power over the governments of the countries in which they operate. In the case of the 'big three', there are many documented instances of the abuse of this power (see box, p.19). Because of their control over marketing and distribution, it has been very difficult for national governments to attempt any independent action aimed at securing a better deal from them. The most renowned example of such an attempt was in 1974 when Panama, Costa Rica and Honduras, decided to impose an export tax of US$1 on each box of bananas exported. The result was a confrontation with the banana companies which has been called 'the banana war'. The companies resorted to all kinds of tactics in opposition to the tax. They reduced the volume of bananas they exported and even suspended all exports in some cases. They also refused to resolve wage negotiations with local unions, and bribed government officials. The tax was subsequently reduced to US$0.20 per box. The governments of Colombia, Costa Rica, Guatemala, Honduras and Panama then set up the Unión de Países Exportadores de Banano (UPEB) in September 1974.

UPEB has tried by various means to increase revenue from banana production. Costa Rica, Honduras and Panama managed to pass new laws which enabled them to renegotiate the terms of their contracts with the multinationals. Export taxes did become an important part of government revenues in these three countries and in Guatemala. However, the aim of a US$1 per box export tax was only achieved in Costa Rica in 1981; but pressure from the companies to recoup the costs of rehabilitation after the wind damage of 1983, led to a reduction in the taxes in all three countries in 1984.

The formation of UPEB and the exporting countries' attempts to increase their earnings led to a decrease in the participation of the multinationals in direct production. But it was difficult for them to withdraw rapidly from fixed investments established decades earlier. Strategies for withdrawal would be difficult to reverse. The companies have put much of their efforts into reducing export taxes or claiming rebates following natural disasters, rather than hastily dismantling their plantations.

The Central American countries have also tried various forms of state intervention to increase their revenue from banana production, including state banana projects, many of which collapsed within five years. In a number of cases, governments overestimated the potential profit margins; the big companies make profits from high volumes at relatively low margins per unit. The state companies lacked the experience and expertise of the multinational banana companies. UPEB also set up its own regional marketing company, the Comercializadora Multinacional de Banano (COMUNBANA) which, in the late 1970s and early 1980s, sold bananas mainly from Panama to Yugoslavia, but it too virtually collapsed in 1983.

The COMUNBANA experiment reflected the difficulties in

challenging the big companies' long-established control over marketing and distribution. This is, however, where many of the profits from banana exporting are made. Access to it would undoubtedly increase the income of the exporting countries, as a study of the exporting arrangements of the Windward Island banana industry by the Commonwealth Secretariat (1981) cautiously pointed out:

> The aim of greater participation by banana-exporting countries in the marketing and distribution of their produce cannot be isolated from the wider implications of the United Nations' call for a new international economic order. Often foreign companies have been able to circumvent national policies or render them ineffective precisely because the exporting countries possessed little or no market information and had limited bargaining power. These comments are not made to belittle the work of the major importing companies, but what is generally sought is a more commodious arrangement for banana exporting countries to participate in the trade, and a more equal balance of benefits between exporting and importing countries.

The banana exporters who operate in the open market face a broader problem due to the competitiveness of the market, which would exist even if they had more control over the industry. Expanding output by each country increases competition between them, leading to problems of oversupply. Predictions for the future suggest that the market outlook for bananas is stagnant or shrinking; one country can only make gains if the market share of another decreases. Only the lowest cost production units could survive in the longer term. In this sense policy options for open market suppliers are very different to those available to the preferential market suppliers such as the Windward Islands. The latter do have room for expansion in their markets, as their main problem has been one of production rather than market access.

While banana exporting countries have faced great difficulties in improving income from their exports, the large companies have done rather well in overcoming problems of low profit margins and the market limitations of their industry. They have concentrated on increasing efficiency rather than sales. The evidence shows that in common with other tropical commodities, notably rubber and tea, there has been a decline in real world prices for bananas between 1950 and 1974. This represents serious problems for the exporters; the volume of bananas which must be produced in order to buy a given quantity of manufactured imports increased 2.5 times over this period. In other words, 10 tonnes of bananas would purchase a tractor in 1950; by 1974, 25 tonnes were required. Although prices recovered somewhat in 1980, they are still very unstable. The 'big three' have been able to sustain an economic rate of return over this period through innovations aimed at reducing unit costs and increasing productivity.

The companies' vertical control enabled them to insist on the use of technology which would increase their share of the final retail price. Better management techniques in the 1960s gave the multinationals new opportunities for improving their efficiency. The introduction of computers to analyse and coordinate harvesting and production schedules, transport and market demands, enabled managers to control operations more closely. Capital investment and improved production methods have also helped the companies overcome market limitations. Disease control, in particular, has been a major objective of investment as bananas are particularly vulnerable to a number of pests and plant diseases (see chapter 3).

The power of the big companies which dominate the industry contrasts with the vulnerability of the exporting nations. From Honduras to Dominica, small, impoverished countries can do little to improve their incomes from a product which renders its greatest returns to those who control its transport and marketing. They remain mostly locked into the production of a commodity which guarantees some foreign exchange and employment, but are unable to generate sufficient surplus to improve living standards significantly. While some countries have managed to reduce their dependence on the banana crop, it still plays an important role in many third world economies. In the case of the Windward Islands, dependence is at its most acute. The following chapter explores the history of Geest in the eastern Caribbean and the nature of its relationship with the region's banana producers.

The international banana industry: future prospects

A FAO study of the world banana economy in 1986 produced a rather gloomy report for the industry's prospects. World imports of bananas have stagnated over the last decade and it is unlikely that there will be growth in the future. The western European market contracted by 10 per cent between 1973 and 1982. World imports decreased by five per cent per annum on average over this period, excluding only the US, whose market showed some signs of growth. The present situation in the banana industry is close to what is called 'maturity'. In other words, it has almost reached saturation levels of demand with little prospect of further growth through increased consumption per head; sales can only increase with population growth. Individual companies may be able to increase their sales marginally through brand name promotion (eg United Brands' *Chiquita*), but this requires expensive advertising to persuade customers that they are better quality than any other bananas. Otherwise generic advertising such as the British 'Bananaman' campaign can attempt to appeal to a general change in attitudes, but the success of such promotion is difficult to gauge. The future for those operating in the open market is therefore not optimistic.

UK banana sources
(boxed tonnes)

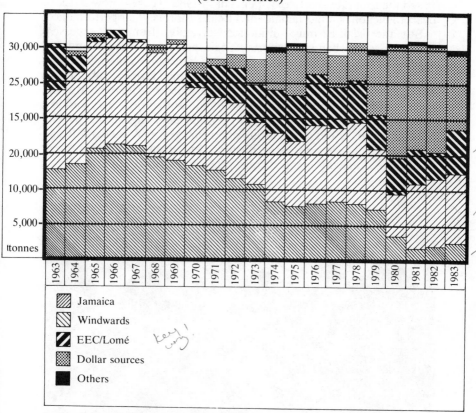

Source: Fruit Trades Journal, April 1985
Note: Since 1983, the Windwards' share of the UK market has gradually increased, reaching 61 per cent in 1986.

For those working with preferential markets, such as the Windward Islands, there is still room for increasing output. The third Lomé agreement signed in December 1984 between the EEC and ACP (African, Caribbean and Pacific) countries, reaffirmed preferential conditions of access and gave special mention to 'improving the conditions under which the ACP states' bananas are produced and marketed' through aid provision. The UK's domestic consumption of bananas has stabilised at around 300,000 tonnes a year, of which the Caribbean (Windwards, Jamaica and Belize) supplied 50 per cent in 1984. Following the introduction of fieldpacking, the Windward Islands raised their market share to 61 per cent in 1986. There is now a risk of overproduction, should Jamaica and Belize improve their performance.

But the islands must ultimately diversify from an excessive dependence on banana exports. Their protected market and the readiness of farmers to accept a regular cash income (although banana production gives a very unfair return for the small farmers' labour) has not encouraged the pursuit of alternative sources of income. But the banana industry remains vulnerable to climate and disease, and is a risky business for the majority of small farmers engaged in it. The present boom could provide an opportunity for Windward Island governments to consider diversification, but given their commitment to *laissez-faire* economic principles, they are unlikely to grasp it.

East London market

2 Geest: Paternalism and profits

The early years: from bulbs to bananas

The popular image of the Geest organisation is of a traditional, benevolent, family business that risked all to break the banana giant Fyffes' monopoly of UK imports, while at the same time stepping in to rescue the ailing economies of the Windward Islands.

Although it does not have the reputation of companies such as United Brands, Standard Fruit or Del Monte, with their widely known use of 'dirty tricks' to maintain their economic interests in Central America, Geest has not got where it is today just by 'being nice'.

Legend has it that two ordinary young Dutchmen arrived in Britain with their bicycles in 1935 to sell flower bulbs. In fact, Jan and Leendert van Geest came to sell exports from their father's well-established market gardening company, Waling van Geest & Zonen of s-Gravenzande, near The Hague. The van Geest family had been involved in the business since 1897 so the young van Geests had considerable backing for their new enterprise.

In the same year, John and Leonard van Geest (as they later became known), formed Geest Horticultural Products Ltd with £2,000 capital; a not inconsiderable sum at the time. They bought land and based themselves in Spalding, Lincolnshire because of the area's suitability for market gardening and its proximity to the North Sea port of Boston. While continuing to import produce from the Netherlands, they also began to grow their own.

Within a year they had set up a distribution network for bulbs which they then used for fruit and vegetables as well. They later expanded into manufacturing and light engineering because of their need for particular types of equipment and agricultural machinery.

The company grew rapidly, changing its name to Geest Industries in 1949 to reflect its new status. By 1950, turnover had reached £4 million and Geest was becoming a major distributor of horticultural products, fruit and vegetables in the UK. It was the company's entry into the banana industry in 1952, however, which was to provide the cornerstone of its development into one of Britain's largest private companies.

The move made sense; Geest already had a national distribution

27

network and importing experience. But two other factors were of much greater importance in ensuring the success of the enterprise: British government policy in its Caribbean colonies and the state of the UK fruit market. Far from being a blind leap into the unknown, Geest's expansion into the banana industry was actively encouraged and safeguarded by the British government.

The 1930s and 1940s had seen a rising tide of social and economic discontent and, more significantly, increasing trade union organisation and agitation in Britain's Caribbean colonies. The development and expansion of a banana industry in the region was largely a calculated response to this unrest on the part of the colonial administration and allied business interests.

We have no bananas

The other factor which made the development of the banana industry the perfect colonial solution, was the state of the UK banana market. World War II disrupted the UK's banana imports which were shipped by Fyffes from Jamaica. Food rationing and import controls persisted until the early 1950s, with banana imports still only about half their pre-war level. In the House of Commons an active 'banana lobby' kept up pressure on the Ministry of Food to resume imports to cater for post-war demand and sustain companies' profits.

The 'banana lobby' was associated with the West India Committee, established in 1775 by merchants and planters trading in the West Indies whose aim was to maximise profits and safeguard trade. Its members had originally been mainly sugar barons but later included 'every important person or firm... engaged in or wanting to engage in business in any of the West Indies' colonies'. Its method of operation was summarised in 1963 by the then Chairman, J A C Hugill: 'We do a tremendous lot of work behind the scenes, much of which is better not talked about, but on the whole we think we serve the West Indies best by doing it in this fashion'.

The open lobbying of Parliament and the behind-the-scenes activities of the West India Committee led to the announcement of a special licensing agreement for the import of bananas in 1953 by the Board of Trade.

Quotas, tariffs and a guaranteed market

Under this arrangement, bananas were classified into two types by their country of origin; those from the 'sterling area', ie countries of the Commonwealth (in particular Jamaica and the Windward Islands) and all others, termed 'dollar bananas'.

Sterling bananas could be imported under an open general licence but a quota system operated on dollar imports, requiring the issue of special dollar licences. These licences could only be issued if demand could not be met by sterling bananas. In addition, dollar bananas were subject to a 20 per cent tariff.

The market for sterling bananas was guaranteed by the quota system of dollar licences. Banana imports from Jamaica in the 1930s and 1940s had enjoyed a protected market in order to help stabilise Jamaica's economy, and in the early 1950s, to conserve sterling at a time of crisis for the pound by reducing dollar imports to the UK. Thus the precedent of a guaranteed market was already established. All that was required was a British company to come and take advantage of this golden business opportunity.

The quota and tariff system for Windward Island bananas has survived international agreements under the General Agreement of Tariffs and Trade (1957), Britain's entry into the EEC (1973) and the three Lomé Conventions (1975, 1979 and 1984), and remains in force to this day.

Geest buys its way in

The Swift Banana Company had briefly produced the Gros Michel variety of banana in St Lucia from 1925 to 1927. In 1931 a Dominican merchant found a market for bananas in the UK and shipped Gros Michel to Liverpool. In 1933 the Canadian Buying Company, a subsidiary of United Fruit, agreed to buy fruit from Dominica and St Lucia on condition that it did not have to deal with individual growers. As a result, the banana growers associations (BGAs) were born to act as an intermediary for the importing company.

In 1934 as a result of Panama disease, the Caribbean banana industry switched from Gros Michel to the Lacatan or Puerto Rique variety of Cavendish bananas. By 1937 the Windward Islands and Trinidad were harvesting more bananas than one ship could carry and the company instituted quality controls, accepting only higher grade (more fingers per hand) and unscarred fruit. Thus began the concern for fruit quality, the implementation of inspection and more care in the transport and husbandry of the crop.

The Canadian Buying Company shipped fruit to Montreal until 1942 (when its 'Lady Boats' were destroyed by German submarines in World War II). The rapid growth of the industry meant that a good number of people now depended on it, so the British colonial office

29

subsidised production in the Caribbean during World War II by paying for bananas which could not be shipped. During these years, individual local merchants found small and less secure markets in Florida, but could not match the organisation and transport facilities of United Fruit and its production in Central America and Ecuador.

Before World War II, Jamaica had supplied 60 per cent of the UK banana market, but exports were curtailed both by the war and the ravages of Panama disease. Following the war, Jamaica was unable to increase production quickly enough to fill the gap in the UK market, nor could other traditional suppliers such as Brazil and the Camerouns. The Windward Islands were relatively free of Panama disease at this time, and some British businessmen were quick to see the potential of the region.

Messrs Foley and Brand had been involved in the fruit trade in Northern Ireland. In 1948 they went to Dominica, bought some land and started growing bananas for export. They formed a company, Antilles Products Ltd, and in 1949 offered to buy and ship all exportable quality bananas produced in the Windward Islands. In 1950 Antilles Products Ltd signed a 15-year contract with the island's growers and began shipping bananas to the UK.

Initially, Foley and Brand used the excess capacity in ships which were taking Jamaican bananas to Britain. Later, they chartered two 16.5-knot refrigerated ships from the Swedish line AB Atlantafik. The company was committed to buying bananas but still did not have adequate shipping capacity to export them.

The Swedish ships called on a monthly basis, which was too infrequent to be reliable for the export of rapidly ripening bananas. In the early days, bananas had to be brought from the other islands to Dominica for shipping. Later, ships often bypassed St Vincent when there was insufficient inward cargo. In addition, the principal market at the time was the US, where Antilles Products Ltd had to compete with the established trade in Central American bananas.

Antilles Products Ltd found itself in financial trouble and without the capital to buy its way out. In 1952, with support from the British government and the West India Committee, Geest bought out Foley and Brand's interests in Antilles Products Ltd and the remainder of the contract with the banana growers.

Membership of the influential West India Committee was essential to smooth Geest's entry into the banana industry. According to George Miller, who worked for the Committee for many years, John and Leonard van Geest only joined just before they took over Antilles Products Ltd and 'from nowhere', were soon elected onto the Executive Committee.

The British government now had a reputable, thriving British

30

company to act as an agent for its colonial policy. Preferential access to the UK market, potential government aid to the Windward Islands' banana industry and an exclusive, watertight contract guaranteed Geest's future prosperity. The interests of the banana farmers of the Windward Islands appeared to come a long way down the list of priorities. The British government had ensured that control of the developing banana industry and the islands' future economic and political stability rested entirely in British hands.

Thirty years of expansion: minimising risks, maximising profits

In recent years the Windward Islands have suffered the effects of the oil crisis, the onset of world recession, falling exchange rates and two major hurricanes. They have each suffered varying degrees of political instability and economic crisis since independence in the 1970s. Geest, on the other hand, has flourished. Its strategy of minimising risks has proved very successful; the key to this is its contract with the banana growers.

The takeover of Antilles Products Ltd gave Geest contracts with the Banana Growers Associations (BGAs) on each of the four islands. It also inherited the estates that Antilles Products Ltd had purchased. The contracts specified fixed prices to be paid by the company for the bananas: four cents per pound until 1953, four and a half cents for 1953-54 and five cents for 1954-55. Geest had exclusive rights to buy and ship all exportable quality bananas produced in the Windward Islands which it maintained until 1955 when the company negotiated a new contract which gave it an even more advantageous basis for determining the price paid to the banana growers. In addition, Geest managed to pass on the burden of the entire cost of the company's shipping operation to the growers. This contract has since been renewed periodically with only minor changes and remains fundamentally intact today as a three-year rolling arrangement. Through its terms, Geest has been able to control the Windward Islands banana industry for 30 years to its own considerable advantage.

Instead of a fixed price agreement, a 'Green Market Price' (GMP) was negotiated which became the main point in the pricing structure. The GMP was the price at which green bananas were sold and delivered to the ripeners' depots in the UK. It had to take into account the fact that ripeners, distributors, wholesalers and retailers (all but the latter came to be controlled by Geest itself) had to make a profit out of bananas. All Geest's costs (shipping and handling the bananas up to the point of delivery to the ripeners) plus a substantial profit

31

margin, were deducted from the GMP. The balance was the price paid to the BGAs.

The price was based on an estimate of the average wholesale price of ripe bananas and was supposed to be influenced by the volume of fruit available on the market, the demand at a particular price and seasonal factors.

With its market guaranteed, Geest saw the potential for an integrated importing and distribution structure which could make a profit at each stage of the process. Geest owned no ships in the mid 1950s, these had to be chartered. The company had no ripening facilities either, these were controlled by Fyffes and scores of other companies. It owned no wholesale or retail outlets, but did have a distribution network in the UK. In the following years Geest rapidly expanded, setting up and buying a range of companies engaged in

Quality control at Geest's former ripening plant, Burnham

ripening, storage, transportation, marketing and wholesaling throughout the UK.

Geest now operates two of its own refrigerated ships and two more on a long-term charter. Outward bound, Geest exports British goods (including banana yoghurt!) to Barbados and the Windward Islands and offers luxury cruise facilities to 12 passengers. Its UK ripening centres handle 80 per cent of the bananas imported from the Windward Islands. The company owns one of the UK's largest fruit and vegetable wholesalers, Francis Nicholls Ltd, and distribution is handled from 11 regional depots by a fleet of 350 trucks. Geest does not own any retailing outlets but supplies all the major high street multiple stores.

In the course of 25 years, Geest and the other major banana importers, Fyffés and JAMCO, have taken over and now control most of the wholesale fruit and vegetable firms in the UK. In the 1960s there was a brief struggle between Geest and Fyffes for larger shares of the British market which became known as the 'banana war'. Geest first of all 'encouraged' Windward Island farmers to increase their supplies (and thus lower prices); the farmers feared that Geest could find other suppliers if they did not comply. The UK market changed in 1963 however, when West Cameroon opted to leave the Commonwealth, thereby losing its preferential access to the UK market. A production and price war ensued between Geest and Fyffes who both hoped to replace Cameroon's share of the market with Caribbean bananas. Jamaica and the Windwards soon captured 95 per cent of the UK market and the two companies have since kept their respective market shares reasonably stable.

Geest operates in such favourable conditions that it has never had to be cost conscious. Any inefficiencies in Geest's handling of the bananas, for example, means that growers have to face extra costs. It is always assumed that damage to the fruit occurs either in the fields or during transportation to the Windward Islands ports and is therefore the grower's responsibility. It is never suggested that bananas could be damaged en route to the UK. In fact, Geest's operation has been subject to some criticism which has suggested that its ships, specially designed for the company, are not perfectly suitable for the transport of bananas. Critics maintain that the ships have excess crane capacity, are faster (and therefore less fuel efficient) than they need be and that their loading/unloading equipment is less mechanised than is required to maintain quality control standards under severe competition from Central American production. It is no accident, these critics say, that Geest ships were among the first to be requisitioned by the British navy for service in the Falklands/Malvinas war. Indeed, it is said that there is a conflict between Britain's Ministry of Defence — which appreciates

33

Geest's excess capacity and its availability to a dwindling UK Merchant Marine — and the Treasury, which would like to see greater efficiency and lower prices for the British consumer. As Geest companies control each stage from the quayside of the Windward Islands to the retailers in the UK, it appears to have had little incentive to cut costs as these are all paid for by the growers.

The Growers' Associations

Since 1958 the Windward Islands Banana Growers Association (WINBAN) has been responsible for negotiations with Geest on behalf of the growers. In the scale of power within the industry, WINBAN and the growers' associations it represents, come well below Geest.

Each island has its own growers' association: Banana Growers Associations in St Lucia and St Vincent; the Banana Cooperative Society in Grenada; and the Banana Marketing Corporation in Dominica. The associations' functions include:

● purchasing all export quality bananas from individual growers
● boxing, delivering and selling to Geest
● controlling diseases which affect bananas
● organising and administering the banana extension service (technical advice)

The associations are statutory bodies whose boards comprise government appointees and elected farmers. This management structure has tended to work in favour of the larger farmers, who usually end up as the elected representatives. In St Lucia, for example, the Board of the Association is comprised entirely of large growers who are able to ensure that the provision of services by the association works to their advantage. Credit, for instance, is more easily available to the wealthier farmers through their influence in the associations.

In the case of Dominica in the mid-1970s, only those growers selling more than one tonne of bananas per quarter to the association were then entitled to subsidised fertiliser from it, in accordance with the quantity of their sales. The association incurred fertiliser costs which were double the receipts from the cess (deducted contribution paid by all farmers), thus subsidising one group of producers over another. Small growers represented over half the total number of farmers selling to the association but their sales were less than 10 per cent of the total purchased. Lack of access to fertiliser, as well as credit and technology, undoubtedly contributed to the lower productivity of the small farmers in Dominica. Their yields were only 0.48 tonnes per acre compared with 3.74 for large growers and 1.84 for medium growers

(CCAR 1978).

The associations' finances are notoriously precarious. Because of the terms of the contract with Geest and despite the protection WINBAN is intended to offer, the growers can bear the brunt of rising costs, losses on exchange rates and natural disasters. But the management structure of the associations has not encouraged cost-consciousness. The larger farmers are keen to maintain their privileged access to services as this increases their return as growers and they do not tend to prioritise reductions in overall costs. The associations' representatives are likely to be satisfied with the maintenance of costs at 'reasonable' levels, since these are automatically paid to them before payments are made to the growers. In addition, like Geest, the growers associations are guaranteed a share of the Green Market Price to cover their costs such as hurricane insurance, price stabilisation contributions, office and boxing plant costs, pest control, WINBAN contributions, export duty etc. Again there appears little incentive to lower these costs and increase the share of the Green Market Price going to the farmer.

WINBAN was formed to represent the growers' interests in negotiations with Geest. Its tasks include:

● negotiating the market and shipping contracts for bananas
● monitoring contracts
● representing the growers on the UK Banana Trade Advisory Committee in London
● initiating research and giving technical assistance to growers
● purchasing inputs needed by the growers

Despite the extent of its functions, WINBAN has always been understaffed, underequipped and underfinanced. It has been in an invidious position from its inception. Set up under the colonial administration, it was part of the British government's plan for preserving British interests in the islands. It has had to represent the growers' interests but at the same time, could not afford to antagonise Geest. As the islands' economies came to depend increasingly on the banana industry, WINBAN has been dominated by the fear that Geest would pull out if its profits were not sustained. WINBAN's attitude to Geest therefore appears to be one of gratitude to the company for its presence. This attitude is well illustrated in the following extract from its 1964-65 Annual Report:

> These tokens of cooperation and assistance to the Windwards banana industry from the buying company have been at the insistence of Mr John van Geest and clearly demonstrate his kindness and genuineness of purpose towards the Windwards industry. There is no doubt that the Windwards have in turn been profoundly grateful.

WINBAN and the growers' associations seem to be, wittingly or unwittingly, allies of Geest. This is likely to be encouraged by the considerable interchange of personnel between the associations and Geest. This 'cross-fertilisation' as the industry defines it, is called 'incest' or a new form of the 'house slave' phenomenon, by others. A former St Lucian chairman of WINBAN is now an employee of Geest. Similarly, a member of Geest's Board of Directors worked in WINBAN from 1963 to 1977, and was at one point head of Research and Extension for WINBAN. A former quality control officer in WINBAN now works as a quality control officer for Geest. In Dominica, a member of Geest (WI)'s board of directors and the island's largest grower, was elected to the Board of the Dominica Banana Growers' Association.

Trips to the UK, fetes, gifts, kickbacks on the bulk purchase of agricultural inputs, all have been alleged at one time or another to have encouraged the cooperation of WINBAN and the islands' individual associations with Geest. Similarly, the 'clubby' atmosphere of the weekly London meetings with Geest and the UK Ministry of Agriculture to determine the Green Market Price, cannot help but remove WINBAN representatives from the reality of the farmers' situation in the Caribbean. Indeed, a recent inquiry at the WINBAN office in London revealed that they neither receive nor keep such basic cost data as is available in the Annual Reports of the islands' growers' associations. In this context, the concern for corporate margins and consumer interest are likely to dominate over the needs of the poor subsistence farmer of the Windwards.

Critics of WINBAN's role also allege that the organisation's research work is not geared towards the interests of the small farmer. The recommendations which have emerged from WINBAN research into quality improvement are perceived as irrelevant to the farmer, but as advantageous to Geest and other multi-national companies with interests in the industry. According to Geest Industries' technical advisor and former WINBAN fruit quality expert, Francis Leonce:

> WINBAN research continued to be very much in the forefront of banana research centres which were working hand-in-hand with prominent chemical manufacturers... to test the commercial effectiveness of new materials.

These manufacturers — ICI, Bayer, May and Baker etc — together with Geest, have contributed to WINBAN research with a view to increasing their commercial stake in the banana industry. By 1979 WINBAN's annual research budget had risen to over EC$1 million.

The small farmer, effectively excluded from participation in WINBAN policy, is unable to afford the inputs generated by such research. This fact was recognised in a St Lucia government report of 1980 which noted that WINBAN's scientific programme had shown 'a deficiency over the years in the area of economic analysis of recommendations' in relation to the small farmer. WINBAN research may therefore benefit Geest and the other companies which sponsor it and the larger capital-intensive grower, but it does little to confront the problems of the smallholder with strictly limited resources. Furthermore, this research has not been properly coordinated with related work by the islands' Ministries of Agriculture and CARDI (the regional research organisation of the CARICOM countries), leading to a waste of resources.

On 1 January 1984 the Green Market Price was replaced by the Green Wholesale Price in a bid to relate the price more directly to the actual UK market and demand than to the cost of production. It is based on the average wholesale price of the bananas received by Geest's ripening centres. Geest then deducts certain charges (freight, handling etc) from the gross green wholesale price to arrive at the net green wholesale price which is the price received by the growers' associations. These deductions account for a significant proportion of the gross price and remain controversial. For the week ending 8 February 1984, for instance, the difference between the gross and net prices was approximately £172 or 37 per cent of the gross offer. Furthermore, the price paid to the grower is still less than the Green Wholesale Price, since the BGA deducts a sum for the range of services which it provides to the grower. In the case of St Lucia, the 1983 gross Green Market Price averaged about EC$0.77 per pound, while the net price paid to the SLBGA was EC$0.42 per pound, and to the growers, EC$0.18 per pound (World Bank, 1985).

While the system was supposed to guarantee better prices for the growers, Geest still has considerable room for manoeuvre. For example, Geest also sells bananas to independent ripening centres and charges higher prices because they are not owned by Geest. These prices are not included in the calculation of the Green Wholesale Price, so the benefits are lost to the growers and Geest keeps the profits. The price Geest pays fluctuates from week to week. Even if the Green Wholesale Price increases in real terms, moreover, it is still possible for the farmer's income to decrease, due primarily to changes within currency exchange rates. This problem is more fully discussed in the following chapter.

Land

From the outset, Geest was a reluctant landowner in the Windward Islands. But in order to show good faith and to encourage farmers to turn to banana production, the company kept the estates inherited from Antilles Products Ltd, and subsequently bought more land. By 1971 Geest owned some 10,000 acres. Although Geest has stated that substantial ownership of land in the islands by a British company was 'inappropriate', the company's main concern, in fact, was to avoid the many risks involved with banana production.

The strategy of building a monolithic distribution and marketing structure allowed Geest to maintain effective control of the industry without becoming a major employer on the islands with its associated risks and management and labour costs. All the risks of crop failure due to disease or disasters such as hurricanes or volcanic eruptions are borne by the growers and not the company.

Bad publicity

Geest's strategy of selling land where possible to the islanders was reinforced by a nine-month strike by workers on their Portsmouth Estate in Dominica in 1978. In October 1977 the Dominica Amalgamated Workers Union submitted a claim to Geest for a 10 per cent pay rise back-dated to 1975 and improved living and working conditions for its members. They had not had a pay rise since 1974. The *Sunday Times* of 13 August 1978 described one worker's living conditions as 'drab and stark... less than 10 feet square. The cooking facilities... are primitive. There is no running water, there is no electricity. There are no sanitation facilities'.

Conditions on the estate were appalling, but this was the norm for the industry. Geest paid its workers just above the legal minimum rate. Edwin Koense, an executive member of the Latin America Congress of Workers (CLAT), visited the estate and commented: 'British farmers would not keep their pigs in some of the hovels Geest workers have to live in'.

Geest's response to the union's claim was considered a derisory offer and was swiftly turned down. The workers went on strike and the company sacked them, hiring others in their place.

The strike lasted nine months during which time Geest was accused of using 'dirty tricks' to try and break it. Allegations included cutting off water supplies, threat of eviction and harassment by Geest's local management. The allegations were denied by the company who claimed that 'it had brought prosperity to the Caribbean'.

The *Sunday Times* also raised the question of whether British companies trading internationally had a responsibility to raise the standard of living of their workers. Geest's reported response was that they did not.

Geest was clearly embarrassed by the adverse media coverage of its operation in the Windward Islands. Within one week of the *Sunday Times* article appearing, the company settled the strike with an immediate pay rise of 15 per cent and a promise that living standards would be investigated.

The final sell-off

Geest finally ceased its own banana cultivation operation in the Windward Islands in September 1983. The company sold some of its remaining land in St Lucia to St Lucia Model Farms Ltd, a new project comprising a series of smallholders who are now farming it. Geest has retained a one-third financial interest in the scheme, the rest of the finance coming from the Commonwealth Development Corporation and the European Development Fund. Geest, meanwhile, retains approximately 2,000 acres in St Lucia, but does not produce bananas there.

St Lucia's Prime Minister has referred to the transfer of land back to the islanders as 'a quiet revolution in the history of St Lucia, whereby the descendants of former slaves who have worked the land for generations are now owners'. But critics of the project have noted the vulnerability of the growers once the initial aid runs out.

The encouragement of small landholdings over the years has not only protected Geest from financial risks but has also added to the strengthening of political 'stability' in the islands. Smallholders are more isolated from one another than plantation workers on larger estates. Being owners, they are also more likely to see themselves as having a stake in the islands' economic system. There is therefore less likelihood of political organisation against the company or the respective governments.

A safe harbour

Geest's dominance over the economies of the Windward Islands and the livelihood of the workers employed in the banana industry has a knock-on effect for dock workers and their communities in the UK. In order to protect its banana shipments and profits, Geest has played off dock workers at Avonmouth and Barry against each other.

Up until 1980 Geest's shipping operation to and from the Windward Islands was based at Barry docks in South Wales. Geest was happy with industrial relations there, as it had signed a 'no strike' deal with the dockers, who were not Geest employees. But the company experienced difficulties in docking its new, larger vessels, and temporarily moved its operation to Avonmouth, which had better facilities.

At Avonmouth however, Geest found industrial relations not to its liking. Registered dockers and lockgatemen were involved in a series of lightning strikes over threats to their jobs, and Geest began diverting ships back to Barry docks in February 1984.

Geest then sought strike-free guarantees from the workforce before returning to Avonmouth. The 1,100 registered and non-registered dockers did in fact agree to a 'protection of service' agreement; this meant that in the event of a strike, they would work on any Geest ship in port at the time as well as the following two ships. The port's 20 lockgatemen however, refused to sign away their fundamental trade union right to strike.

Under such circumstances, Geest was not prepared to base its shipping operation at Avonmouth; the workforce was too militant. The company finally managed to negotiate a further 'no strike' deal with Barry's dockers with a promise to return there permanently. With the aid of a £250,000 grant from the Welsh Office, Geest had a new £1 million handling terminal built to cater for its large ships at Barry, and is now hoping to avoid industrial unrest with a more compliant force of dockworkers.

The Economic League

Perhaps a more sinister aspect of Geest's relationship with trade unions has been its financial support for the Economic League, a right-wing anti-union organisation based in London. From 1972 to 1981, Geest donated over £6,000 to help finance the League in its claim to 'monitor revolutionary organisations… every working day of the year — and not a few weekends when extremists often hold their meetings to plan further trouble for industry'.

The League's activities include 'screening' workers who apply for jobs in industry, publishing anti-union material, running courses for management and, up until 1983, providing consultancy services. At its peak in 1978, the League supplied personnel managers with details of over 400,000 workers whom they had 'screened' and distributed over 18 million leaflets to shopfloor employees. Since then, however, its activities have declined, as restrictive government policies have taken their toll on Britain's labour movement. It is interesting to note nonetheless, that during 1978, the year of the Geest plantation workers' strike in Dominica, Geest's annual donation to the League increased from the usual £250 or £350 to £1,000.

The 1986 Geest Annual Report notes that of the £11,005 donated to charitable and political organisations, 'no political contributions were made'. It is unclear as to whether the Economic League is defined for these purposes as 'political', and it is not known if Geest continues to contribute to the organisation.

Geest PLC

In 1986 Leonard van Geest junior, chairman of the company since 1980, stood down from this position but remained chief executive. His successor was Charles Bystram, formerly managing director of United Biscuits International. At the same time, other senior executives from a range of companies were brought into Geest. The company was now preparing for the next stage in its development.

Geest had already got rid of some of its loss-making peripheral activities, such as the computer subsidiary, which was sold in 1984. It was concentrating on its profitable distribution business, spending almost £8 million on a new depot at Maidstone and £1 million on upgrading its national stock control system. This return to the company's basic activities in fresh produce and allied areas, together with changes in senior management, heralded the flotation of Geest shares on the London stock market in November 1986. At this point in its 50-year history, Geest could claim to be Britain's ninth largest private company, with a turnover of £372 million in 1985.

The share offer was massively oversubscribed, reportedly by 20 or 30 times. More than 100,000 applications are thought to have been received with 25.6 million shares on offer at £1.25 each. The flotation raised £32 million; its purpose had been to attract new capital investment for the company's expansion and development, as well as to sell off a substantial proportion of direct family interests. The Geest family are reputed to have received some £23 million in the process. Among investors was the Kuwaiti government investment organisation, engaged in a 'stake-building' operation. Despite the influx of new shareholders, however, the Geest family naturally maintain a majority and controlling interest in Geest PLC.

The 1986 Annual Report following the company going public, announced a pre-tax profit of £9.1 million, based on pro-forma continuing activities. This figure represented a 39 per cent increase on the 1985 profit. A contributing factor was a rise of 26 per cent in the sale of bananas, based on increased production in the Windward Islands. The report also noted that Geest was expanding its export business to the islands because of their 'improving economies'. The company was therefore in a position to take advantage of a profitable two-way shipping service.

As a thriving public company, Geest is now able to diversify into

Loading bananas on to 'Geestland', Kingstown, St Vincent

Roshini Kempadoo

more lucrative activities and divest itself of loss-making concerns. It is currently anxious to increase its share of the prepared food market in Britain and to strengthen its distribution service to the various multiples. To this end, Geest took over the Clipper Group, a fish products company in July 1987, for the sum of £10.2 million. At the same time, it has shed parts of its unprofitable horticultural sector, selling off its interests in houseplants. So far, Geest's share price has not risen dramatically within the context of a buoyant stock market. It remains to be seen how the company will attempt to expand in the highly competitive market for prepared foods.

Mutual dependency?

At the centre of Geest's development has been the import of bananas from the Windward Islands, based upon the contracts between the company and the BGAs and the protected UK market, last formalised in the Lomé Convention of 1984. The company's steadily rising turnover (see table) has largely been based upon these factors.

Growth of Geest's corporate turnover	
Year	Size of turnover (£m)
1950	4.0
1970	68.0
1972	80.0
1974	116.8
1979	220.5
1981	268.8
1984	337.8
1985	371.9
1986	421.1
Sources: CLAT-Nederland, Geest Annual Reports	

Whether Geest still depends upon this arrangement for its continuing success, however, is open to debate. The Offer for Sale, published in the *Financial Times* of 17 November 1986, observed that the present licensing system would be reviewed in 1988 and that if it were not to be renewed, it would expire on 28 February 1990. It also remarked of the contracts with the BGAs that 'the Directors see no reason why [they] should not continue for the foreseeable future, for the benefit of both the Islands and Geest'.

However, the document goes on to conclude:

> It is not possible to predict the effects of the Convention not being renewed or the contracts not being continued substantially in their present form. However, the Directors believe that Geest's position in the banana market is not dependent solely on either the Convention or the contracts, but is underpinned by its expertise in the banana market, its investment in infrastructure (which would be expensive for a competitor to replicate) and its customer base.

In other words, Geest implicitly suggests that it could continue to function as a banana importer without the long-established connection with the Windward Islands. This is presumably to attract potential investors who might otherwise be concerned at the prospect of the company losing its preferential market. Or it could simply be a coded message to WINBAN: 'don't rock the boat'.

Under existing conditions, Geest has no reason to abandon its operations in the Caribbean. The banana industry is undoubtedly profitable for, as one competitor observed at the time of the flotation, 'when it's going well, it's a licence to print money'. Yet at least Geest does have the option of pulling out of the Windward Islands and would doubtless contemplate doing so if economic or political developments dictated such a move.

The people of the Windward Islands have no such freedom of choice. If Geest withdrew from the region, an already precarious economy would effectively be destroyed. The Windward banana industry could not compete on the open market with Central and South American producers, and the vital cash lifeline to small farmers would be broken. Ironically, it seems likely that the Windward Islands need Geest more than Geest needs them, even if most of the profits from bananas have always found their way to Lincolnshire rather than to the Eastern Caribbean.

3 Banana work: How the Caribbean farmer earns his 'ten per cent'

A risky business

The banana farmer of the eastern Caribbean receives little more than ten per cent of the final retail price of his (or her) produce. Even this figure is misleading, since the farmer must subtract the costs of fertiliser and pesticides, any labour hired, tools etc, before he has anything to spend on food, clothes and other basic necessities for his

---

Who are the banana farmers?

Accurate statistics and social surveys of the banana industry in the Windwards are very rare. The following data comes from T H Henderson and P I Gomes: *A Profile of Small Farming in St Vincent, Dominica and St Lucia. Report from a baseline survey* (Agricultural Extension Department, University of the West Indies, St Augustine, Trinidad, 1979). It provides some indication of the basic features of small farming on the islands.

Dominica

(Sample of 120 farm units of 1-5 acres)
Of farm operators:

82% were male
70% were between the ages of 41 and 70
62.5% could read and write
6% had secondary education
50% had completed at least 4 years of primary school
20% had no formal schooling

50% said that their only occupation was farming
12% were skilled tradesmen
10% were in agricultural related commercial enterprises in retail trade of farms produce
20% were in fishing and unskilled work of different kinds. ▶

---

family. This chapter looks at what is involved in banana production, what the farmer does to earn his 'ten per cent'.

The land must be cleared and drained before planting and holes dug. Bananas grow in a wide range of soils, but require good drainage and at least 25mm per week of rainfall (2,000-2,500mm per year) for satisfactory growth.

The farmer must decide how many suckers to plant in a given area. Much will depend on the fertility of the soil and the amount of money the farmer has for fertiliser over the year; other factors such as availability of labour and alternative uses for the land will influence his decision. Bananas are often planted as a shade crop for other nursery or tree crops such as cocoa or nutmeg. The farmer's field plan must take into account the needs of these inter-cropped plants which are usually long-term investments, taking up to five years to bear fruit.

The farmer then has to buy the suckers or clones of good quality banana plants. Each plant produces about five suckers, although this can be increased to 10 or even 20, in nurseries especially prepared for propagation. The amount of disease and pests and the yield and quality of fruit from the farm which sells the planting material as well as the

---

The majority spent 6-8 hours a day in farming activities during cropping season, otherwise only 2-4 hours. 80% had help from the family. 41.7% relied on shared labour.

75% used fertiliser, but only 25% used chemical sprays and less than 1% used other chemicals.

50% lived up to 10 miles, 15% lived 11-20 miles and 105 lived over 20 miles from the nearest marketing depot.

Farmers were fully utilising all land available to them; 120 farmers operated 234 parcels, one third of it freehold.
30.8% of the land was family land
15.0% paid an annual rental
6.4% sharecropped
6.0% squatted on government land

The land available was on the least accessible mountain slopes of interior with heavy soils.

85% cultivated bananas
43% cultivated coconuts

The basic diet was root crops and bananas. Over 90% consumed these from their own cultivation. They also ate fish and had milk, both of which had to be bought several times a week.

They identified their needs as better roads, electricity, water supplies and health care. ▶

---

actual price of the suckers, will all effect the economics of production for the farmer. Another consideration is the relative stages of growth of the suckers. Uniform size and type will produce a crop at roughly the same time. This may or may not be desirable depending on the farmer's cash flow needs throughout the year. The time of the year at which the fruit will be mature enough to harvest is also important as prices are cyclical and tend to be higher in the summer.

The farmer must soak the suckers he has bought in pesticides such as Jebegon, Aldrex, Aldrin and/or white lime to kill nematodes and borers. Nematodes are an almost microscopic, worm-like boring pest which reduces the ability of the roots to take up nutrition and water from the soil. In addition to impairing the roots' function as a channel for plant nutrients, the damage caused by nematodes can allow fungus disease into the root and otherwise weaken the root system, making the plant more susceptible to wind damage. There may be as many as 13-30,000 nematodes on a pound of banana root. There are other ways of getting rid of nematode infestation such as fumigation of the soil or dry fallowing of infected fields, but they are all relatively expensive.

The suckers are then planted about 25-30cm into the soil. Their root

---

St Lucia

(This was a handpicked sample by an extension officer; farmers had an acreage of 1-15.)

95% were male
The average age was 47 years
60.8% literacy

70.8% only occupation was farming
97.2% use fertiliser
49% used chemical sprays
19.8% used other agricultural chemicals.

50% were between 5 and 10 miles, and one third were 11-20 miles from the nearest marketing depot.

88.3% grew bananas, 88.3% cultivated cocunut, 65.8% grew breadfruit and 56.7% grew citrus.

Bananas were planted mainly May to July, with sizeable minority planting all year round.

St Vincent

(Sample of 120 farm units of 1-5 acres)

70% were male
50 years was the mean age ▶

---

system is therefore rather shallow and weeds are a great problem. Herbicides are used to get rid of the weeds, though a cheaper method — slashing them down with a cutlass or machete — is the more usual method for the poor farmer.

Bananas require large amounts of mineral nutrients if they are to produce good yields. But the small farmers of the Windward Islands cannot afford the necessary quantities, and yields are therefore lower than on Central American banana plantations, for example, where very large amounts of potash fertiliser are applied.

Nematodes, banana borer and weeds are not the only dangers to the banana plant. Other pests, in particular leaf spot and Moka disease, are major problems. Leaf spot is a fungal disease which attacks the banana leaf, resulting in poor yields, reducing bunch grade (the number of fingers on each hand) and the size of the individual fruit; it also causes premature ripening of the fruit. It is controlled by regularly spraying the leaves with a fungicide either by air or by hand from portable backpack sprayers. In Dominica the majority of the banana crop (about 60 per cent) is sprayed by hand, whereas in St Lucia rather more is sprayed by aircraft, as a greater proportion of the crop is grown

---

72% literacy

64% only occupation was farming
70% used fertiliser; less than 20% used chemical sprays.

Only 30% cultivated bananas, but these were planted and harvested all year. Majority preferred short-term rather than long-term crops.

Problems of access to marketing depot rather than distance. Small farmers farmed the steepest and least accessible land.

Conclusions from surveys

The small farmer population of the Windward Islands was middle-aged (40 years and over) and had 60-70% literacy. Labour available from their households made a significant contribution to the operation of small farm agriculture. They lived on staple foods of root crops and bananas, which were home grown. Land and labour were the most heavily employed resources. Farmers looked upon land as 'a scarce and precious resource to be guarded jealously and utilised as carefully and efficiently as their knowledge and experience will permit'. Family help and shared labour were used for a majority of farm tasks, though labour was sometimes hired for drainage and weed control. 95% of farmers in St Vincent and Dominica had five or less hand tools which were their only farm equipment, and there were no farm buildings. 70% of farmers in St Vincent and Dominica, and 60% in St Lucia, made no use of credit facilities; there was very low investment.

---

on estates located in river valleys convenient for aerial spraying.

Moko disease is a bacterial wilt of the banana and is spread by infected cutlasses, shoes, vehicles, plant material, insects, etc. It is

Farmer throwing fertiliser pellets, St Vincent

Roshini Kempadoo

becoming increasingly serious in the Caribbean. Plant health measures are necessary to control it, such as the disinfection of tools, shoes etc as well as the treatment of diseased root mats.

Apart from the control of weeds, diseases and pests, the farmer must also prune the banana trees to prevent excessive growth of bunches and suckers on each plant which will reduce the size and yield of the fruit. Once the bunches have 'shot', they are often covered with a plastic sheet to prevent even the slightest scratching by birds, insects and blowing leaves which may result in discoloration when the fruit eventually ripens on the supermarket shelf or in the kitchen of the legendary 'scrupulous British housewife'.

The bunches must be supported as their weight might cause the plant to collapse prior to the stage when they are harvested — about two-thirds before maturity. WINBAN and the growers' associations sell special cord for this purpose, but few of the farmers can afford to buy it and they use their own makeshift methods.

There are clearly a multitude of factors which the farmer must take into account in banana production. But there are a whole range of environmental factors, such as soil quality, climate and water, which are outside his control, though they considerably increase the risks to his livelihood. There is also another series of difficulties related to the harvesting and transport of the banana crop. The banana is a soft fruit and therefore easily bruised. But it does not show damage in the green stage when it is harvested. The long period between cutting the bananas in the Windward Islands and delivery to retail stores in Britain (about 22 days) is full of risks of damage which will result in discoloration and therefore reduced market appeal. As well as physical damage which can be caused in this way, staining from sap released during cutting and fungi can damage the appearance of the fruit.

The farmer must therefore take a number of precautions to prevent damage. The harvesting and selection of bananas for export is very rigorous. As much as 40 per cent of the crop can be rejected as unsuitable for export. Traditionally, bunches of bananas were carefully cut from the tree and carried wrapped in old banana leaves, straw or styrofoam pads, to the nearest road for collection and delivery to the closest boxing plant. Each bunch was usually carried on the head for some distance due to the lack of feeder roads in many parts of the islands and the small farmers' lack of cash to pay for motor transport.

Boxing plants used to play an important part in the long process of getting this vulnerable fruit to its eventual market. On arrival at the plants, the banana bunches were 'dehanded' that is, each hand of 14 to 18 bananas was separated from the bunch (there are 6 to 11 hands per bunch), and poor quality or damaged fruit rejected. The hands to be

Loading bananas for transport to docks, Grenada

boxed were then weighed and washed. The flowers on the fruit were removed and the hands dipped in a fungicidal solution before being packed into cardboard boxes for transport to the docks and eventually, the ripening sheds in England. The majority of workers at the banana boxing plants were women.

Fieldpacking

In 1983 Geest, in association with WINBAN, began promoting field packing as a way of avoiding the damage caused by transporting bananas to the boxing plants. Under this system, the bananas are packed in plastic boxes so close to the banana plant itself as to eliminate any damage. By the end of 1986, this system had been adopted for almost 100 per cent of Windward Island banana production. Boxing plants were closed and many jobs were lost. Most have been turned into Inland Banana Depots, distributing the boxes to the farmers. Farmers must fill a minimum of 70 boxes; smaller farmers have to club together to fill the quota.

The scheme has been hailed as a great success. Production has increased markedly, helping the islands to recover their position in the UK market following Hurricane Allen. Most of this has been attributed to the improved quality of bananas resulting from field packing. Dominica's exports rose from 28,518 tonnes in 1983 to an estimated 60,575 in 1987. In St Lucia, production rose from 53,787 tonnes in 1983 to an estimated 118,456 in 1987. There was even a 23.5 per cent rise in production in 1985 and the 1986 shipment, despite a storm in September which devastated 15 per cent of the farms on the island, was the largest ever. In St Vincent and the Grenadines, production increased from 27,267 tonnes in 1983 to an estimated 48,301 in 1987; in 1986 the September storm devastated 55 per cent of the island's farms, but exports were still 38,000 tonnes for the year. Grenada, the smallest producer, shipped about 9,700 tonnes in 1987, compared with 8,500 in 1983.

Total Windward Island exports to Britain have risen from 66,000 tonnes in 1980 (following the destruction by the hurricane), to 118,000 tonnes in 1983, 137,000 tonnes in 1984 and 167,000 in 1985. In 1986, exports reached a record 200,000 tonnes (see graph).

Most small farmers have, of course, been well pleased with the success of field packing, basically because it means more cash in hand. They have planted more land with bananas as a result. However, in Dominica, the small farmers' union has pointed out that they do not in fact get their proper payment for the extra work involved (see box). Boxing the bananas in the field is hard work on the hillside farms where many small farmers live. But the farmers tend not to calculate the costs

Windwards production 1982-87
(tonnes)

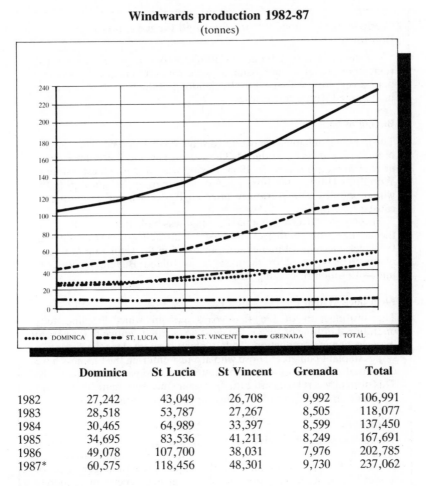

	Dominica	St Lucia	St Vincent	Grenada	Total
1982	27,242	43,049	26,708	9,992	106,991
1983	28,518	53,787	27,267	8,505	118,077
1984	30,465	64,989	33,397	8,599	137,450
1985	34,695	83,536	41,211	8,249	167,691
1986	49,078	107,700	38,031	7,976	202,785
1987*	60,575	118,456	48,301	9,730	237,062

* Forecast

Source: WINBAN

of their extra labour when working out their earnings. It is difficult to make any generalisations for the islands as a whole, however, since there are widely differing employment practices both within and between the islands. The present boom has increased the demand for labour; women previously employed at the boxing plants can earn relatively well, although irregularly, as field packers.

Despite increased production, the Windward Islands have still not realised the full benefit. The price of bananas is denominated in

53

Fieldpacking — a view from the small farmers' union of Dominica

'The banana industry has undergone a series of changes. Some of us still remember the days when bananas were sold on bunches. During that period very little was given to the handling of the fruit. Bananas could be accepted with a few bruises.

Boxing of bananas

The handling of bananas moved to a stage further in 1961, when boxing of the fruit was first introduced. The experiment was shelved because it proved to be too costly. In 1966, boxing was tried on Geest Estate at Woodford Hill but the boxed bananas arriving in Britain during the winter months were seriously affected by 'crown rot' — a disease caused by a fungus.

In 1969, the DBGA's first boxing plant was built at Rosalie. By 1971, the change from stem fruit to boxed fruit delivery was completed. Considerable sums of money were invested in the setting up of boxing plants. Today, most of them serve as Inland Buying Depots; an underutilisation of existing structures.

Field pack system

The introduction of the field pack system which became fully operational in June of 1986 is the most powerful incentive to farmers to increase banana production. Today, many farmers clear the mountain slopes to plant bananas. Those who are just entering the business have the initial difficulty of access to inputs like fertilisers and chemicals. This difficulty is relaxed after the first year since systematic deductions are made from sales to provide for inputs in the future.

Hard work

The farmer no doubt receives more money today. But, have we stopped for a while to weigh the amount of work involved in the production of bananas? Or are we blinded by the appearance of larger sums of money? In comparison to previous years, farmers receive more money today but they also work much harder. Farmers are engaged not only in the production process but also have to do the necessary handling and packaging right on his field. What was too costly for Geest and the Association is now passed on to the farmer. The farmer does the work that the boxing plant workers used to do but for less than half the money.

Who gets the lion share from the field packing system? The intermediaries (Geest and DBMC) are the ones who cut the cake, leaving the smallest piece for the farmer. They are the ones who determine how much the farmer gets for his labour. The farmer is faced with a situation of take it or leave it.

▶

Inefficiency

Now that banana production has surpassed the figure of 50,000 tons, attempts should be made to improve the efficiency of the operations at Fond Cole. It seems that farmers' time is not even being considered when one talks about costs and the benefits of the field pack system. It is tiring for the farmer to be in the field all day and to spend the night waiting to weigh 100 boxes of bananas. What about the smaller producers; are they getting large amounts from banana sales? The people who really get benefits from the field pack system are the farmers who own well in excess of 5 acres of land. The land tenure pattern in Dominica shows that the majority of farmers own less than 5 acres of land.

Geest has managed with the field pack system to guarantee its supply of bananas from the Windward Islands. He has gone much further in St Lucia where they have introduced the 'model farms'. The time will come when they will try similar experiments in Dominica.

Cut back on exports

Farmers, in response to the calls made by the DBMC and DBGA are now producing much more bananas than before. Although the United Kingdom Market has the capacity for 320,000 tons of bananas, this market has the tendency to contract during the winter months. This is usually a period when farmers' production are at its best. What is being done by the DBMC and DBGA to assist farmers to avoid this problem?

Winter conditions in the United Kingdom has forced Geest to cut back on exports. What is the farmer going to do with his excess production? WINBAN needs to do something positive in that direction. Now, more than ever there is need to look for new markets to sell our bananas.'

Source: Dominica Farmers' Union Newsletter, January 1987.

Eastern Caribbean dollars and is therefore subject to the prevailing fluctuations in the pound sterling/EC dollar exchange rate. Until 1976 the EC$ was pegged to sterling at a rate of EC$4.80. In 1976, however, the then Eastern Caribbean Authority (now the Eastern Caribbean Central Bank), under pressure from 'tourist islands' such as Antigua, switched to the US dollar. In the 1980-81 period, the EC$ averaged EC$6.00 to the pound, due to sterling's strong position against the US dollar. The fall in the value of the pound in 1983-84, however, meant that the rate fell to just over EC$3.00 per pound at the end of 1984. Hence, although Dominica increased its exports by almost 9 per cent between 1983 and 1984, it increased its earnings by only 4 per cent, from EC$23.9 million to EC$29 million. St Lucia estimated its losses in

Fieldpacking in Grenada

56

1984 from the falling pound to be EC$20 million. The British government has, however, rejected calls from the Windward Island governments for a 'banana pound'.

Another problem facing the small farmers is that wintry weather in Britain has affected the distribution and marketing of bananas. But the winter months are often the most productive for the farmers. However, in January and February 1987 Geest declared it could not take all the bananas produced. In Dominica it made a complicated arrangement which few small farmers understood, announcing one week that it would only buy 60 per cent of whatever they had supplied the previous week.

From port to shop

At the port, samples are taken from the boxed shipments and a further round of quality selection takes place. The boxed fruit is weighed and kept in sheds at the port until it is loaded onto refrigerated ships for transport to Britain.

Unless they are cooled within two days of cutting, bananas will ripen quickly and be more susceptible in this softened state to damage as well as to attack by fungus. Research has suggested that a mild acidic bath could prolong this to four days. However, at present, strict timing is required to ensure that the delay between harvesting and loading on the refrigerated banana boat is less than two days. Local radio stations advise farmers of the arrival time of ships. The banana boats used to arrive every fortnight, although now it is usually weekly. The tradition of the 'fortnight' has become a significant feature of island culture, as the arrival of the boats also meant payment for the farmers.

Once loaded onto Geest's refrigerated vessels, the fruit is kept at a constant temperature until it is delivered to their warehouses in England. Geest stores, ripens and handles the wholesale distribution of 85 per cent of Windward Island bananas in Britain, selling only a small percentage to independent ripeners. For the ripening process, bananas are held at 21 degrees Celsius and 90-95 per cent relative humidity for one or two days, followed by four to six days at 18 degrees celsius. They are also treated with Ethylene gas to stimulate ripening. Geest receives about 19 per cent of the retail price for its part in the ripening of bananas, almost double the farmer's ten per cent.

Geest's fleet of 600 or more trucks then distribute the fruit throughout the UK to retail outlets. In a Vincentian newspaper article in January 1977, a Geest spokesperson proudly noted that Geest's trucks were on every high street of every town in the country on almost every single weekday.

Who takes the risks?

From this brief description of the stages involved in taking bananas from the field to the high street shops, it is clear that bananawork is a risky business. But it is the banana farmer who bears the costs of the industry to the point of delivery to the ripeners, receiving a very small return; it is the farmer who takes the risks. In the present boom conditions, he will have no complaint, but it is the farmer who may see his income wiped out by a hurricane. Geest can merely substitute Windward Island bananas with those from Central or South America.

4 Case studies

This chapter looks at the banana industry in three of the Windward Islands; St Lucia, Dominica and Grenada. It also examines briefly the collapse of the banana industry in Jamaica, which illustrates many problems associated with banana production.

The most detailed case study is from St Lucia, based on a study commissioned by LAB from David Demacque, the chief agricultural officer of the island. Many of the problems raised in this case study also apply to the other islands.

Our other case studies contrast two attempts to 'modernise' and 'restructure' the banana industry. In Dominica, the conservative government of Eugenia Charles has followed the path advocated by USAID, whereas in Grenada under the government of the New Jewel Movement (1979-83), efforts to regenerate the banana industry were part of an overall programme of social transformation and economic diversification of the island. The Grenada case study is based on a study commissioned by LAB from the Grenadian economic historian, George Brizan.

St Lucia

We [St Lucia] have inherited our export economy in which the very operation of the economy was geared to external and not domestic demands and needs. The best resources in our countries were utilised for producing the export staple... Whatever resources remained, which were very few in both quantity and quality, could not satisfy our domestic requirements. The result was a large import bill and a disincentive to local production fostered by an attitude which maintained that foreign goods or anything with a foreign label was superior to our local products...

The basic problem associated with the import/export economy lay also with the nature of our exports and imports. Our exports are primary products like bananas which suffer from the vagaries of the weather and sensitivity of their prices to factors outside of our control... Our imports, on the other hand, are high valued goods, covering every category from food to capital goods. A simple calculation will show that with every passing year, we have to export an increasing number of bananas in order to import a single motor car. In 1975, it took 13 tons of bananas to buy one

1,200cc Datsun. In 1980, it took 16 tons of bananas to buy the same car. Our imports are also bought from a wide variety of sources and of necessity in relatively small quantities. We therefore have no control over the supply prices.'

Prime Minister, The Honourable W Cenac, New Year's Address, 1982

St Lucia is a volcanic, mountainous island with a tropical climate; it lies in the path of hurricanes, especially during the months of August to September.

In 1983 its population stood at 126,600 of whom over 65 per cent were 24 years and under. The youth of its population results in a large labour force; official government statistics put the total economically active population (between the ages of 16 and 65) at 45,500 in 1983, ie 36 per cent of the total population. But the economy cannot provide sufficient jobs for those able to work. The World Bank estimated unemployment at 20-25 per cent of the labour force in 1984. It is probably nearer 35 or 40 per cent, if the large number of people who are under-employed are included. In some rural areas, especially those distant from commercial centres, unemployment may be as high as 75 per cent.

Agriculture has played the major role historically in the country's economic development, dominating the lives of the St Lucian people.

Land distribution in St Lucia
(1961 and 1973/74 census)

Size (acres)	Number of holdings		Net percentage
	1961	**1973-74**	
less than 1	4,606	4,750	+ 3.12
1-4	6,130	3,750	−38.82
5-49	2,119	1,732	−18.26
50-99	63	44	−30.15
100-199	38	26	−31.57
200-499	33	30	− 9.09
500-2000+	19	17	−10.05
Total	13,008	10,349	

Note: The 1973/4 census is misleading. Sixteen estates covering 4,082 acres were not enumerated up to 1975. The explains the reduction of holdings in 1973-74.

Source: Rural Transformation Collective, 1979

The importance of this sector and, in particular, the banana industry to the economy, is further enhanced by its role as the major source of employment on the island; 39.5 per cent of the working population are engaged in agriculture, which contributes almost 14 per cent of GDP.

Scarcity of arable land in this mountainous country, is a major problem for agriculture. Only about 9 per cent of the land area is believed to be arable (14,000 acres), of which 86 per cent (12,000 acres) are under banana cultivation. The importance of the sector hinges on the role of export agriculture. Despite some efforts at diversification, banana production still contributes almost 50 per cent of domestic exports. In 1984, they earned US$20.4 million out of total merchandise export receipts of US$43.7 million. The World Bank estimates that the banana industry injects almost EC$1 million into the economy every week. Over half the population are directly dependent on it.

Apart from bananas, coconut is the second most important export crop; income is derived almost exclusively from copra (used in oil extraction). Like the banana industry, coconut production has also been seriously hurt by climate. In 1980, Hurricane Allen reduced production from 6,000 to 2,500 tonnes per year; it was estimated that complete recovery would take five to eight years. Production is also hampered by difficulties in getting labour for harvesting and drying as well as poor farm access roads and rat damage.

Other tree crops grown in St Lucia are cocoa, coffee, nutmeg, avocado, mango and citrus. These are grown throughout the country, but not in sufficient quantities or concentrations to provide adequate economies of scale in their harvesting, marketing or processing.

Yam, dasheen, sweet potato and tannia are the staple foods of the island and are grown widely on small farms throughout the country, frequently interplanted with bananas or other crops. Yields are low, although tannia and dasheen were once exported to the UK and neighbouring islands. The island also grows perennial spice crops, but there is no strong tradition in spice cultivation. Ginger is the most important crop and is exported to the UK. Vegetable production has expanded since the late 1960s, but the problem of maintaining regular supplies and linking production to the export market and tourist trade remains unsolved. Hotel operators claim that domestic produce is too expensive, supplies are not regular and a good variety of product is not always available.

There is some potential in livestock production on the island, although at present it is a small-scale industry. Commercial livestock production contributes less than two per cent to GDP and demand for most meat and dairy products is met by imports. Feedstuffs are also not available locally and protein supplements or commercially-formulated animal feeds must be imported. The St Lucia Flour Milling Company at Vieux Fort manufactured mixed animal feeds, but damage to the mill and to crops by Hurricane Allen in 1980 led to the closure of the mill.

Domestic food production remains the most disadvantaged agricultural sector. It suffers from a chronic lack of financing, as most resources are channelled into export agriculture. Marketing institutions are also all geared to export crops. In the domestic sector, production is disorganised and haphazard. Marketing problems, low production and declining and fluctuating seasonal market prices, have forced the farmer to cultivate only small amounts of food which can be easily sold. There is a rush by food producers to get to market early and catch the higher prices, which leads to a glut of food on the local market.

Joyce Cole (1980) found that it is the degree of organisation, at both national and farm level, which is responsible for the progress made by the banana industry. In contrast, the low level of organisation in the domestic sector is related not only to the low development of this sector itself, but also to the lack of education of small farmers, their low living standards and poor perception of the world outside and of themselves as a group. A large percentage of rural dwellers also form the greater part of the 20-30 per cent illiteracy which exists. All these factors affect the application of science and technology to increase domestic food production. Farmers are fairly resistent to change and slow to innovate even when they have resources.

The small farmer in St Lucia mostly finds himself on the sidelines of development, which has wide implications for the overall progress of the island's economy. Preference and tastes for imported food products will persist as long as the domestic sector — the small farmer community — is unable to produce replacements and substitutes in adequate quantities and standards. Food imports are a major consumer of scarce foreign exchange. Other related effects are the rural-urban drift, the readiness to emigrate and the lack of technically oriented individuals in the farming business.

Incomes are very low on the island. A 1980 study found that the 'majority of small farmers earn less than US$400 per farm family annually from farming activities and this is below the subsistence level'. These farm households amounted to 42 per cent of the total population. A large proportion of the island's urban and rural population have an inadequate diet. A 1974 food and nutrition survey by the Caribbean Food and Nutrition Institute showed that half the households consumed less than 80 percent of the calories necessary for good health. Part of the problem is that the main sources of carbohydrate (rice, root crops and flour) and protein (fish and meat) are imported and beyond the purchasing power of many families. It has been estimated that 66 per cent of the total food energy supplies, 100 per cent of the cereals and about 80 per cent of the meats are imported.

Tourism and export-oriented industries have in recent years begun to make significant contributions to the island's economy. Tourism has become the major foreign currency earner (US$41.1 million in 1984). But, as elsewhere in the Caribbean, it remains an enclave industry. The luxury, mostly foreign owned, hotels, contrast sharply with the poverty of most of the island's inhabitants.

Foreign investors have been attracted to both tourism and manufacturing in St Lucia, partly because of the low wages. In 1985 an electronic assembler earned US$0.80 per hour. The industrial sector began with the establishment of a carton-manufacturing plant in the 1970s; subsequently some 70 manufacturing operations were set up, producing clothes, plastic products and soft drinks. By 1974 clothing and paper industries had captured 13 per cent of exports and the export of agricultural products declined from 100 per cent in 1970 to 75 per cent in 1979.

Progress was nevertheless fairly slow, despite generous tax incentives. But from 1984, the Caribbean Basin Initiative gave preferential access to the US market for certain products from the region. Eleven new ventures were established between January 1984 and May 1985, creating 670 jobs. A recent study by the Economist Intelligence Unit suggests that export-oriented industries will enjoy growth rates averaging 10 per cent over the next five years and together with tourism, will keep growth in St Lucia on average at above four per cent per year (Burgaud, 1986).

Critics point out, however, that both tourism and export manufacture are patterned on the needs of foreign capital rather than on those of the St Lucian people. The sector on which most St Lucians will continue to depend is agriculture, and this has yet to make the important and much needed link with the rest of the economy. US aid programmes have been unable to establish such links. Indeed, they have in the past undermined policies which could benefit the development of agriculture, for example, regional integration. Before the overthrow of the NJM in Grenada, USAID deliberately excluded that country from its aid programmes, such as the multi-cropping research programme of the Caribbean Agricultural Research and Development Institute (CARDI).

Recent data on the island's economy suggests growth coupled with deep structural problems related to its over dependence on agriculture, particularly bananas. Since 1981 the growth rate of real GDP in St Lucia has been positive, if fluctuating. In 1984 it was five per cent, the highest over the previous six years, reflecting the recovery of tourism and the banana industry. This recovery has not, however, had much impact on unemployment, which has increased in recent years as the construction industry has slowed down.

Fiscal deficits have traditionally been a problem on the island, where central government plays a considerable role in economic life. In fiscal year 1984/85 the deficit amounted to 4.3 per cent of GDP, an increase from one per cent over fiscal year 1980/81. The island suffers from persistent balance of payments deficits which have widened over the years. The current account deficit was US$12.3 million in 1975; by 1980 it was US$47.4 million. This reflects the poor performance of the country's economy over those years, but also its open nature, resting so crucially on imports and exports. Tourism, manufacturing and the associated construction and service sector, all have a high import content. Food imports rose from EC$7.2 million in 1967 to EC$52.2 million in 1979, ie 19 per cent of total imports.

More recently, while the current services balance has been positive due to a 33 per cent increase in receipts from tourism between 1980 and 1984, the trade balance has remained negative. The latter has outweighed the services balance resulting in a persistent current account deficit, despite significant remittances from St Lucians living or working abroad. The most recent figures (1987), point to a trade deficit for the previous year of EC$197 million; food exports amounted to EC$84.7 million against imports of EC$73.0 million.

The external debt has grown from US$8.0 million (19.8 per cent of exports) at the end of 1977, to US$42.3 million (49 per cent of exports) in 1983. The government has had considerable problems in servicing this level of debt, going into arrears a number of times.

The weakness in the island's terms of trade reflects its high dependence on bananas. The banana industry remains of overwhelming importance to the island's economy.

The St Lucian banana industry

A little history

Until the 1920s, and going as far back as the 16th century, the dominant plantation crop in St Lucia was sugar cane. Side by side with sugar, the peasants produced a variety of food crops for subsistence. Limes were also produced on the large estates and by the peasants from about 1910.

Today, St Lucia is the largest producer of bananas in the Windward Islands. In 1983 it exported 45 per cent of the region's total banana exports. It was also the first of the islands to export bananas, beginning in 1925 with the short-lived Swift Banana Company venture.

In 1933 another United Brands subsidiary, the Canadian Buying Company, offered a five year contract to purchase bananas from small growers if they formed an association to handle collection and loading of the fruit. The company instituted similar arrangements with growers in Dominica, Grenada and St Vincent at the same time. However, as with these other islands, Panama disease and transport difficulties during World War II, had liquidated the industry by 1941.

Foley and Brand of the UK (via Antilles Products Ltd), encouraged by the Colonial Office, signed a 15-year contract in 1948 guaranteeing to purchase all Windward Island banana exports. In 1951 the Colonial Office sent a team of three experts to provide technical assistance and to help with the establishment of the St Lucia Banana Growers' Association (SLBGA) as a private company. By 1954 the SLBGA had 1,055 members and branch offices throughout the island. Any farmer with at least 30 plants could become a member, and any 15 members could form a branch. Antilles Products was then sold to Geest in the early 1950s.

Banana production expanded in St Lucia in the 1950s as sugar production declined. Sugar had survived longer on the island than elsewhere in the region. In 1961 the van Geest family negotiated the purchase of two estates and sugar factories, Roseau and Cul de Sac. These were then turned over to bananas although Geest had originally stated that they would maintain sugar production. Considerable employment was lost as a result and alternative supplies of sugar for the local market had to be found at short notice and high cost. GFL Charles, Chief Minister under the colonial administration, describes in the box below his government's consternation at the way Geest accelerated the demise of the sugar industry in favour of bananas.

Geest's change of heart

[By 1961] 'Mr van Geest successfully finalised negotiations with Sugar Manufacturers Ltd for the purchase of the Roseau and Cul-de-Sac Estates and Factories. After the change of ownership, Mr van Geest offered to buy all publicly owned shares which was double the invested value. This offer was welcomed by shareholders as a windfall and within a comparatively short time, van Geest, with a few exceptions, bought out all the ordinary shareholders.

To be able to ascertain the development policy of the new owner, the Labour Government invited Mr van Geest to a meeting, being fully cognisant of the Geest specific interest in bananas. The proposed plan of development as outlined by Mr van Geest was that the cultivation of ▶

---

sugar cane and the manufacture of sugar would continue and that he would operate with one central factory at Roseau which would be modernised and structured for that purpose. Banana cultivation would be introduced in the Cul-de-Sac valley and phased over a period of years so that the greater portion of the valley would be in banana cultivation. To facilitate the quick transportation of sugar cane from the Cul-de-Sac valley to the Roseau factory, not covered for transportation by rail, a new road would need to be constructed or alternatively the widening of the existing main road. He requested and was given Government's assurance of financial assistance in the new road project. The West Coast road which was in fact widened was indeed for Geest purposes.

The Labour Government applied for a Colonial Development and Welfare grant from the British Government to meet the road commitment, but in the meantime it was to be observed that the new Company had prepared lands in the Roseau valley for banana cultivation. The new Company's attention was immediately drawn to this serious variation of the development policy announced to the Government through Trade and Industry Minister, Herman Collymore. At a meeting convened by the Labour Government to discuss the apparent change of development policy in the Roseau valley, the Company assured the Government that only a few acres of the peripheral land were being used for banana cultivation for diversification and that the original plans for sugar cane cultivation and manufacture of sugar would not be altered.

A letter from Mr F J Carasco, Managing Director of Roseau and Cul-de-Sac Estates and Factories, announcing that the sugar crop year 1962 marked the end of sugar production in these valleys and addressed to Chief Minister George Charles, was considered by the Labour Government to be sudden and deliberate. The Company had complained of poor yields, an uneconomic export price, wage demands which could not be met, low turn-out of workers etc... The decision to cease sugar production with such immediate precision cast a dark shadow of suspicion on the assurances so often given to Government that sugar production would continue in the valleys... In this instance, not even the St Lucia Workers' Union which represented the sugar workers was invited to a discussion before a decision was taken by the Company which would change the nature of operation in the valleys.

The Labour Government requested the Company to withdraw its decision to stop the production of sugar during a series of discussions following the announcement, and both sides issued separate press releases for public information. The Company would not deviate from its decision and Government had to find immediate alternatives to supply the public with sugar in 1963.'

Source: G F L Charles, *Struggles of the St Lucia Working Class* (unpublished)

Land ownership and bananas

... [let us] consider the situation whereby the available agricultural land is under the control of 0.17 per cent of all farmers and more so, most of this insignificant minority are absentee owners, and the opposite situation where 92.7 per cent of the farming population control only 23.99 per cent of the available land. It is this opposing state of affairs, together with the archaic land tenure system of multiple ownership, that have created the land hunger which, fuelled by the innate compulsion to survive, has forced large sections of the agricultural workers and small peasants to squat and cultivate unsuitable areas. Their practice of shifting cultivation has embraced the denuding of forested areas and has thus exposed the land to the detriment of erosion and the drastic depletion of water sources and reserves. In this scenario, domestic food production, that is almost exclusively in the hands of the small farmer on the hillside suffers, and banana production for export in the more arable areas also suffers. Erosion of top soil and inadequate water for irrigation are aspects which contribute to low yields in both of these cases.

(David Demacque)

The distribution of land ownership in St Lucia according to the 1961 and 1972/73 census is given on page 60. It is extremely unequal. Small peasants owning less than five acres of land own 82.1 per cent of all farms. Middle strata peasants owning land between five and 50 acres own 16.4 per cent of all farms, while the large landowners form only one per cent of all farms. But when these figures are related to the actual size of holdings, a striking picture emerges. The small peasantry control only one per cent of the farm land area, while the two other categories control 32 per cent and 67 per cent respectively.

The census data shows in fact, that all private property in excess of 500 acres per owner is owned by 17 persons; they own an amount of land equivalent to 47 per cent of land in agricultural holdings. At the other end of the scale, 4,700 small peasants live on holdings of less than one acre. Over the years there has been a greater concentration of landholdings. In the absence of firm legislation on land purchase, there is considerable mobility in the land market. Foreigners have been able to buy up land with considerable ease. Of the eight estates over 2,000 acres at the time of the census, only two were owned by St Lucians. As many as 55 joint stock companies and corporations own land in the big estate sector. Geest owned 40,000 acres of prime farmland until 1983.

Few of the very large landowners in St Lucia use the land for genuine agricultural purposes. Some, especially the absentee landowners, hold the land for speculative purposes in real estate, or as collateral to finance loans for other business activity. Some of the large estates over 100 acres, grossly underutilise their land. Although they often occupy the most fertile land, as much as 55 per cent of the total acreage is uncultivated, compared with 18 per cent on small estates.

The larger estates are responsible for the bulk of banana production. According to the World Bank, only 1,500 farmers are responsible for about 80-90 per cent of total production and a similar volume of exports. The St Lucia Banana Growers Assocation (SLBGA) has a registered membership of 10,000 of which 7,000 are active; so the majority of farmers produce only 10-20 per cent of total production between them. Most agricultural labour is also found on the larger estates, although as one study pointed out:

> ... the number of persons employed by these estates is totally inconsistent with the size of the estates, creating in the process, a large reserve army of unemployed people in the rural areas. Sixty-four estates, over 100 acres employ only 2,260 workers, that is only five per cent of the persons employed in agriculture. This situation obtains as most of the estate lands remain idle.

> (Rural Transformation Collective, 1979)

The low wages and poor conditions on the estates have contributed to the migration of many young St Lucians from the rural areas. Most prefer to seek work in the capital, Castries, or to leave the country every year for seasonal work on US and Canadian farms.

The small farmers

Over 75 per cent of banana farmers have 10 acres of land or less. Much of their land is on hillsides and is poor, marginal land. Laws of inheritance based on the French Civil Code have encouraged the fragmentation of land in St Lucia. The system of family land tenure or multiple ownership arising from these laws, mean that when a single proprietor dies, the land is divided among his heirs, each of whom is entitled to an undivided share in the whole and his right to use the land is not lost even if it is not exercised for a period. Where there are several co-owners, disputes occur as co-owners claim a share of a crop planted by others; it also creates problems for mortgaging land to raise capital or using it as collateral for credit.

Low yields, poor fruit quality and the high costs of inputs have made bananas of very marginal profitability to the small farmer. The pricing of bananas at above world market level has helped sustain the industry, but this may have delayed the search for meaningful crop diversification.

The low yields per acre have made St Lucia, along with the other Windward Islands, a relatively high cost producer. On the few, well-managed large plantations, a return of 10 to 12 tonnes per acre is possible, but the average is 5 to 6 tonnes, compared with 10 to 15 tonnes in the neighbouring French islands of Martinique and

Guadeloupe. This is a result of complex factors. The problem of fragmentation, with farmers forced to cultivate smaller and smaller portions of land, has already been discussed. Much of the land used for banana growing is not really suited to it. But even those peasants with a little more land are often only able to cultivate small portions of their holdings, as family labour, on which they depend, may not be available. Only farmers with considerable resources can hire labour. A traditional system of community help called the 'coup d'main', whereby a number of farmers would help in farm work on the farms of different members of the group in turn, no longer exists.

Lack of access to credit also affects productivity. A survey of 10 per cent of St Lucia's smaller banana growers (25 acres or less) in 1978, found that only about 25 per cent used agricultural credit. Since then, the St Lucia Development Bank (SLDB) was established in 1981 to provide small farmer credit. But problems of lack of security and difficulties in loan repayment still prevent the small farmer from making use of such facilities. The inaccessibility of many small farmers has also made it more difficult for them to receive regular help from agricultural extension officers. Problems with the service itself, such as lack of experienced officers and teaching aids, have also limited its effectiveness for the farmers.

The St Lucia Banana Growers Association (SLBGA)

The SLBGA was formed as banana production began to be organised on a commercial basis. It provides the means through which the actual production of bananas is organised at the farm and national levels, ensuring the growers services in production - fertiliser supply, pest and disease control, other inputs, extension and insurance services — fruit processing and transport. The bananas are produced by the growers, but from the boxing stations (until the introduction of field packing) they become the responsibility of the Association.

The business of the Association is administered by a Board of Directors, composed of growers elected by the Annual Conference of Delegates, and individuals nominated by Government. 'Participation' by the rank and file, is through the 40 branches, where members hear about the business of the Association.

Despite their numbers, the small farmers have found themselves with very little influence within the Association. Indeed, the history of the Association suggests that there has been a deliberate policy to debar their participation in decision-making. The 1980 Commission of Inquiry into the banana industry found that:

> From its inception in 1953 to the time of its restructuring in 1967, the Annual Conference of Delegates comprised delegates elected at branch

level with representation being based on branch membership, allowing one delegate for every 30 members. By 1967, the number of banana growers had risen to approximately 17,000 which meant that more than 500 delegates were eligible to attend and participate in the proceedings of the Annual Conference. It was felt that, apart from providing for a cumbersome meeting, the preponderance of small farmers at the conference provided the risk of domination by those farmers in the management of the Association. In consideration of the foregoing circumstances, Government introduced the Banana Growers Association Act of 1967 which provided for a restructuring of the membership from three categories of growers. Simultaneously, a measure was introduced which allowed representation at the Annual Conference of Delegates by a single delegate for each District Branch. As a result of this latter measure, the Annual Conference of Delegates from 1967 to the present allows participation of a maximum of 40 delegates representing the 40 district branches.

(Government of St Lucia, 1980)

The new arrangements limited the number of growers eligible to represent their branches as delegates, and consequently as candidates for election as directors. Those growers who sell less than 500lbs of bananas per week (90.7 per cent of banana producers), cannot be elected representatives of their branches. The 1980 Commission concluded:

It is clearly an injustice to exclude 90 per cent of the producers in an industry contributing 35 per cent of total output from the decision making process of the industry.

In this way, 10 per cent of Association members, all large growers, came to dominate its affairs. The result was that the small farmer found he lost out in the allocation of SLBGA services, such as transport, disease control, distribution of agricultural inputs, allocation of quality bonuses etc.

The Commission of Inquiry

St Lucian banana production went into a period of crisis in the 1970s following a prolonged drought from 1970 to 1977. Banana exports fell by more than 50 per cent in 1977. The industry came to depend on aid and credit. From 1969 to 1979 WINBAN and the St Lucian and British governments provided the industry with some EC$4.3 million in aid. SLBGA's debt rose to EC$8 million by 1980.

In 1979 political change in St Lucia brought new attention to the industry. The St Lucia Labour Party (SLP) defeated the United Workers Party (UWP) of Conservative Prime Minister John Compton after 15 years of UWP rule (see Introduction). A faction of the SLP led by George Odlum and Peter Josie, had close ties with the New Jewel Movement which had just taken control of the government of Grenada on 13 March 1979, and was pledged to radical changes in Caribbean politics. Odlum attracted considerable support from rural and urban workers, dissatisfied with the previous government's record of corruption and economic mismanagement.

Early in this period of new government, the SLP recognised the crisis facing the banana industry and the inability of the SLBGA to deal with it, and appointed a government Commission of Inquiry. One of the first acts of the Commission was to recommend the dismissal of the General Manager of the SLBGA in an effort to eliminate corruption, inefficiency and mismanagement. The Commission also recommended the expansion of the SLBGA board from nine to 13 members in order to increase the level of participation of the smaller growers in the Association. It called for the dismantling of the:

> ... wall of frustration which prevents 90 per cent of the membership from entering the decision making arena, which sacrifices participation for expediency, which insulates management from the general membership.

The SLBGA board was very hostile to the Commission since most of its directors were affiliated with the UWP. The board had considerable influence on banana growers of all sizes, promoting a so-called 'bond of unity' between growers, irrespective of the differences in wealth and power between them. Its hostility, combined with the attacks on the government by former Prime Minister Compton and his local and foreign business associates, undermined the government's attempts to introduce changes.

The Commission also found that Geest (still a large landowner at the time) had a major influence in the SLBGA as one of the five largest growers on the island and concluded that:

> ... there was a fundamental conflict of interest for Geest to be both 'marketing agent' and 'buyer' of Windward fruit. This conflict must inevitably work to the advantage of Geest Industries and the disadvantage of the producers and their association.

The conflict brought open antagonism between the rank and file members of the Association and members of the Board of Directors who tended, consciously or unconsciously, to look after the interests of Geest.

But political confusion within the government itself further ensured that none of its promises of change were fulfilled. The SLP split when Odlum was denied the Prime Ministership (despite a prior agreement with the SLP leader, Alan Louisy) and subsequently the Odlum faction of the SLP also split. Odlum and two of his parliamentary colleagues resigned from the SLP and formed their own party, the Progressive Labour Party (PLP), but both the PLP and the SLP were defeated in elections in May 1982. The small farmers and workers who had expected to see their lives improve with 'progressive' politicians in office had grown frustrated and disillusioned.

The defeat of those politicians with at least some commitment to reform, laid the way open for the return of conservative Prime Minister John Compton. The priority of the new government was not to seek ways of improving the lot of the small farmer through restructuring the agricultural sector, but to modernise the economy through incentives to private enterprise and foreign investors.

Compton's government has seen the introduction of field packing in St Lucia and the establishment of a system of 'model farms'. The largest estates in the Roseau and Cul-de-Sac valleys have been subdivided by Geest with assistance from the government of St Lucia and the Commonwealth Development Corporation.

The social cost of the banana industry

It goes without saying that the banana industry, and to a relatively lesser extent its predecessor, the sugar industry, have contributed in one form or another to the 'development' of the economy of St Lucia. Bananas have been called a 'social transformer'. There are a number of conspicuous reminders of this, namely, main and feeder roads, ports and other infrastructure which have been built as a direct consequence of banana production and trade. Foreign exchange earned has also gone into the purchase of vehicles and consumer durables.

But this pattern of development has ignored the basic needs of St Lucia and its people. 'Resource misallocation' has also accompanied the growth of the banana industry in St Lucia and resulted in a number of distortions. Foremost amongst these is the persistent and expanding unemployment on the island. The nature of the work involved in banana production on the larger estates means that they are unable to use all available labour all the time. Underutilisation of labour persists in the production of bananas.

The banana industry is going through a period of expansion, and if there are no natural disasters or adverse weather conditions, production could reach over 110,000 tonnes in 1987. Given the lack of arable land, the only way to achieve this increase is through yields per acre rather than acreage under cultivation. As the best land is still controlled by a very few farmers, it will be difficult for smaller farmers to improve their output substantially. Much of their land could not produce more even with the application of fertiliser. Fieldpacking has evidently improved incomes because it has reduced the number of

Small farmer and his house, Dominica

damaged bananas. But land reform is clearly a prerequisite for any real improvement in the lives of the majority of farmers. Improving production based on existing land tenure patterns also contains many dangers for the island's ecology, risking the destruction of hillside forestry. Bananas do not have root systems which hold the soil, and erosion could endanger the island's ecosystem. Ultimately, the way forward for St Lucia, as for the other Windward Islands, must lie in diversification towards a more balanced economy capable of meeting the needs of the majority of the island's population.

Dominica

'There is no room for politics in bananas.' (Prime Minister Eugenia Charles, 1984)

Dominica is the largest of the Windward Islands in area, yet has the smallest population. Largely mountainous and inaccessible, it has an extremely underdeveloped infrastructure and few resources. Despite attempts by the government to attract foreign investment, Dominica remains disproportionately dependent upon agriculture for its export earnings.

Land ownership is markedly skewed, as two per cent of farms occupy more than 50 per cent of available agricultural land. These farms, owned mainly by a traditional plantocracy and covering between 100 and 1,500 acres each, stand in contrast to the holdings of some 4,000 small farmers who work between one and five acres. Sharecropping and plantation wage-labour continue to account for a significant amount of agricultural production.

Fifty per cent of Dominica's population is below the age of 25. The official rate of unemployment is 13 per cent, but the real figure is reckoned to be closer to 50 per cent. This is partly due to the collapse of the lime industry which was sold to the government in 1983 by L Rose, a Cadbury-Schweppes subsidiary, in 1983 and which was subsequently allowed to run down. It is also the result of more general underdevelopment and a long history of governmental inefficiency and corruption. The other major agro-industry in the island is Dominica Coconut Products which manufactures oil and soap for Lever Brothers and Colgate Palmolive.

The provisions of the CBI have as yet failed to stimulate significant foreign investment or generate employment. Manufacturing accounts for less than 10 per cent of GDP, and up until 1985, a mere 148 jobs had been created by CBI-related investment in textile and agro-industrial production. Two industrial parks have been built in the hope of attracting foreign companies to the island. A further incentive to foreign capital investment is the prospect of the lowest assembly work wage levels in the English-speaking Caribbean at US$20 per week. Bananas are consequently vital to the Dominican economy; they currently account for 70 per cent of foreign exchange earnings. The island ranks second in volume of WINBAN exports.

Canada was the first organised market for the island's bananas which were sold to the Canadian Buying Company in the 1930s. Sales were at first controlled by the large landowners who did not necessarily produce bananas themselves, but who acted as marketing agents for the purchasing company. Small farmers were responsible for production and transportation of fruit to the buying point. Production technology was accordingly peasant-based, with few imported inputs. Fruit was sold by the bunch, untreated and unwrapped, and payment was made in cash upon delivery. The only service provided to farmers was information concerning delivery schedules.

The impact of the banana industry on the economy in the 1940s was marginal in comparison with other crops such as limes, cocoa and vanilla. Nor was its effect upon food production negative, since land devoted to banana production was integrated with land used for domestic consumption. Little wage employment was created, as the bulk of production was carried out by families of smallholders.

The arrival of Geest as the purchasing company marked a turning point for the Dominican industry. Large landowners commenced production of the fruit as an estate crop, following the example of the Geest estates inherited from Antilles Products. Bananas ceased to be an exclusively peasant crop, as large-scale production began to compete with peasant intercropping. As exports increased and bananas became increasingly important in the island's economy, the large farmers took control of the Dominica Banana Growers Association (DBGA). The DBGA subsequently became a vehicle for the interests of this minority, providing it with preferential access to vital inputs and credit (see chapter 3).

The Dominica Farmer's Union was formed in 1978 in response to the government's extreme inefficiency in handling the leaf spot control crisis caused by the DBGA. Despite early warnings from WINBAN and the farmers themselves, the virtually uncontrolled spread of leaf spot seriously reduced banana earnings and caused severe hardship for the farmers as well as the nation's balance of payments. In 1979 in the wake of the destruction of Hurricane Allen, a leader of the Farmer's Union, Atherton Martin, was appointed agricultural minister. He was instrumental in organising emergency relief and rehabilitation programmes for a brief period, until Prime Minister Seraphine grew fearful of the power his activities might give to the small farmers and he was removed at the end of the year. The island's banana industry remained in deep crisis for many months. Indeed, for two years after the hurricane, neither the Banana Grower's Association nor the government received any income from banana production.

The election of the Freedom Party led by Eugenia Charles in 1980 signalled a new era for the island. Deeply conservative and pro-American, Charles set up an authoritarian government committed to free enterprise. The repercussions for the banana industry were felt in 1982 when Charles signed an agreement with USAID without consulting the farmers, which turned its most important sectors over to private ownership in return for US$1.8 million in aid over three years.

The move was intended to improve efficiency, but a consultant to the industry revealed that part of USAID's evaluation was based on an erroneous conversion of pesticide usage from US to Imperial gallons, which suggested a much greater level of waste that was in fact the case. The consultant maintained that the DBGA was not particularly inefficient, but that servicing previous debts was causing serious financial difficulties. The farmers union, which mounted fierce opposition to the move, agreed that the management of the growers' association had been inefficient and even corrupt, but did not agree that the answer lay in turning the industry over to large private investors. The union predicted that the USAID project in the banana industry would mean 'two years of sun and sand' for US agribusiness technicians while US accountants remedied the industry's cash flow by limiting credit to farmers, controlling loan repayments, cutting prices paid to farmers and paying them in kind with US chemicals (Dominica

Farmers Union, 1982).

The opposition of the farmers' union forced the government and USAID to back down on the overall plan for the privatisation of the industry. But certain key features have been implemented. These include the separation of all marketing and service functions from the DBGA and their transfer to the new Banana Marketing Corporation. This corporation is ostensibly a private company, but five of its seven directors are appointed by the Minister of Agriculture and the other two are elected by the Dominica Banana Producers Association (DBPA). The DBGA has been disbanded and the DBPA set up in its place essentially as a 'talking shop' for farmers. In fact, Eugenia Charles has been anxious to maintain control over the industry despite her commitment to private enterprise and has tried to ensure at least a right of veto over the appointment of the general manager of the new corporation.

All five staff members of the DBPA are appointed and paid by the government. Their main purpose now appears to be the organisation of branches of the Association throughout the country as an alternative to the Farmers' Union. Only the Association can legally make representation to the government and the Marketing Corporation. Furthermore, to be a member of the Association, a farmer must sell at least five tonnes of bananas per year. Over half the island's banana farmers would be excluded in this way.

Despite the intention, however, the Farmers' Union has gained considerable influence within the Association. The President of the union was elected Chairman of the new Association's branch in the village of Wesley and thus to the Executive of the Association nationally. From there, he was elected by the Association to be one of its two representatives on the Board of Directors of the Marketing Corporation. In many villages, there is almost a 100 per cent overlap between the Association and Union executives.

Since 1983 Dominica's banana exports have risen steadily; from 28,407 tonnes in 1983 to 51,000 tonnes in 1986. This increase in production is largely due to the system of field packing which became fully operational in June 1986. As elsewhere, increased revenue from the field packing allowance has given Dominican farmers the incentive to produce more through expanding cultivation, but this revenue is outweighed by the extra labour involved. Field packing has also led to a loss of jobs within the industry. In 1985 the Banana Marketing Corporation announced the closure of three boxing plants with over 200 redundancies. One woman we interviewed while she was field packing on a steeply sloping smallholding had been made redundant by the closure. She commented that the new system was less efficient and harder than the previous boxing arrangement.

Nevertheless, the Dominican government has praised the 'improved efficiency' of the Banana Marketing Corporation, agreeing to write off a debt of EC$4.9 million in 1986. The Corporation claimed it was a debt which was a legacy from the now defunct DBGA.

Grenada

Grenada ranks fourth in banana production among the Windward Islands, having traditionally been more dependent on exports of nutmeg and cocoa and on tourism for its foreign exchange earnings. From the early 1950s until 1979, its banana production suffered from the same ups and downs as elsewhere in the region. From March 1979 to March 1983 the industry encountered the same difficulties as those of its WINBAN neighbours, but they occurred within the context of a revival of Grenadian agriculture, stimulated by the radical New Jewel Movement government.

From 1934 onwards, along with·the other Windward Islands, Grenada initially sold bananas to the Canadian Buying Company, until shipments were disrupted by World War II. The island's banana exports increased tenfold in the first three years of this arrangement. Production expanded again following the agreement with Geest in 1953. In 1954 the Grenada Banana Cooperative Society (GBCS) was granted the sole right to purchase export bananas from the island's farmers, saving Geest the problem of coordinating production with several thousand small growers. Between that year and 1958, exports grew dramatically by 2000 per cent, from 49,863 stems to 948,000, despite the devastation of all tree crops by Hurricane Janet in 1955. The guaranteed market provided by Geest, together with an influx of aid money for post-hurricane rehabilitation, enabled the industry to recover quickly from the disaster.

Most of the island's banana cultivation was intercropped with cocoa and nutmeg, which had been its principle export crops prior to Geest's arrival. Bananas were found to be an ideal nursery crop for longer-bearing traditional tree crops because they provided both shade and an interim income until the cocoa and nutmeg began bearing fruit some four or five years after planting.

Grenadian banana exports increased to a peak in 1967-68 of almost 2.2 million stems, or 26,575 tonnes. Production then dropped over the following two years, partly due to drought, and partly to the political mismanagement of Prime Minister Eric Gairy. Gairy introduced what he called a 'land reform', which was in effect a means of punishing his opponents by expropriating their estates and distributing them as small, uneconomical plots to his supporters. A number of estates went

77

out of production as exports came increasingly from smaller, less efficient farms. Gairy also neglected the island's infrastructure; the deterioration of feeder roads made transport to the boxing plants and port more difficult and costly.

The setbacks to the banana industry took place against an increasingly vociferous and anti-Gairy political movement which gathered momentum in the early 1970s. In the interests of political stability, as well as economic considerations, Britain formulated and funded a Banana Rehabilitation Plan for the period 1973-76. Under this plan, fertilisers and weedkillers were donated to the GBCS through the Grenadian government and then sold to farmers at half price, while pesticides were distributed free of charge. The 1973 oil price rises had affected the cost of chemical fertiliser so the measures were of considerable benefit to the farmers.

With these subsidies and rising banana prices, export production expanded on the island. Geest took advantage of this temporary period of relative prosperity to change its contract with the GBCS and WINBAN by transferring direct responsibility for the purchase of boxes, hurricane insurance, export taxes and producer bonuses to the growers' associations. Previously, Geest had assumed responsibility for these costs and had charged the associations for them. The objective of this move was to take the rising cost of these expenditures from the farmers' share of the negotiated Green Market Price for bananas; the GMP was not rising as fast as production costs in the industry so the step was of considerable advantage to Geest.

When the Banana Rehabilitation Plan ended in 1976, banana exports fell again as costs rose with the removal of input subsidies. Farmers continued to grow bananas in order to maintain a regular cash income between cocoa, nutmeg and food crop harvests, but they did not grow as much as before.

A new aid scheme for the industry began in 1977, including not only Grenada, but all the Windwards Islands. Unlike the special post-independence programme in Grenada, this plan provided only subsidies for fertilisers and other chemicals, rather than free inputs for the growers associations. The lower effective subsidies, plus inefficiencies in the delivery of services to the industry by WINBAN and the growers' association, did not provide the necessary incentives to increase export production. The additional acreages of cocoa and nutmeg planted during the 1973-76 plan also had an impact on banana acreage; yields were only 3.1 tonnes per acre in 1977-79, compared with 10.6 tonnes during the 1973-76 scheme.

Grenadian banana production thus suffered the familiar vicissitudes of rising production costs and stagnant prices. Even when prices did rise, they never compensated for the greater increases in the costs of chemical inputs after the 1973 oil crisis. The Grenadian farmer had no incentive to invest time and effort in banana production, so yields, as well as the quality of the island's banana production, fell.

The People's Revolutionary Government (PRG), which came to power in March 1979, aimed to revive the country's ailing agricultural sector. It initiated a three-pronged strategy to restructure it: A search for alternative markets (see box); the processing of local produce; and the export of non-traditional products. The establishment of an agro-industrial plant made it possible to utilise local crops which had not

---

Diversification

For us the most important aspect in building an economically independent country (which is the only way that you can truly say that you are politically independent) is the method of diversification — in all ways, in all aspects. First, diversification of agricultural production, secondly diversification of the markets that we sell these products to, thirdly diversification of the sources of our tourism, the variety of countries from which our tourists come. The maximum of diversification, the minimum of reliance upon one country or a handful of countries means the greater your independence, the less able certain people are to squeeze you, pressurise you and blackmail you.

Bernard Coard, Finance Minister in the People's Revolutionary Government of Grenada, July 1979.

---

been fully exploited in the past. Nectars, juices and conserves were produced successfully by the 'Spice Island' plant.

In the case of bananas, however, some of the problems remained beyond the government's reach. As the smallest of the WINBAN producers, and with its WINBAN partners unwilling to seek structural change in the marketing system, it was impossible for Grenada to challenge Geest in any way; the island remained beholden to the company. Banana production remained low after the brief recovery of 1975-76. In 1980, for instance, exports of 11,650 tonnes represented only 44 per cent of the 1968 figure, and 74 per cent in the 1976 recovery year. The hurricanes of 1979 and 1980 were largely to blame for this decline, even though Grenada suffered less damage than its neighbours.

Nevertheless, the new government managed to make significant improvements in the lives of the banana farmers. Investment in agricultural feeder roads improved access to markets for both food and export crops. The government also supported the activities of the Productive Farmers' Union, the Agricultural Workers' Union and other farmers' bodies which lobbied for more credit, improved services, better prices from the National Import and Marketing Board and many other demands. The elimination of the corruption and inefficiency which had characterised the Gairy regime also improved overall agricultural services, such as the distribution of fertiliser and pesticides and disease control programmes.

The PRG had hopes that it could change its banana marketing arrangements through more trade with Eastern Europe and the Soviet Union. While COMECON (with the exception of East Germany) consumes fewer bananas on a *per capita* basis than Western Europe,

---

Jamaica

The growth in Windward Island banana production stands in stark contrast to the dramatic decline of the Jamaican industry. At the beginning of the 20th century Jamaica was one of the world's leading producers and the prime supplier for the whole of Europe. By 1937 the island was providing 87 per cent of total UK imports, and in that year production exceeded 360,000 tonnes. The Jamaica Banana Producers Association, founded in 1929, briefly competed with Fyffes, the British subsidiary of United Fruit, for the export of Jamaican bananas, creating a rival shipping and distribution network. In 1936, however, an agreement was reached which provided Jamaica Producers with 25 per cent and Fyffes with 75 per cent of Jamaican bananas for the UK market.

World War II led to the suspension of exports to Britain, and the industry was only kept alive by substantial support from the British government. Production recovered after the war, even though Ecuador had by now overtaken Jamaica in export output. In 1953 the Jamaica Banana Board began operations as a body with monopoly rights to purchase bananas from growers for resale to exporting companies. This, and various other state-controlled organisations formed a complex marketing structure in which corruption and bureaucratic inefficiency reduced the growers' share of the wholesale price.

In the 1970s and early 1980s the Jamaican banana industry underwent a spectacular collapse. From an export figure of 200,000 tonnes in 1966, volume fell to 107,000 in 1973, 22,000 in 1982, and a mere 11,000 in 1984. While reflecting a more general malaise in the Jamaican economy, the decline in the banana industry was also specifically accelerated by the catastrophic hurricanes of 1979 and 1980.

The electoral victory of Edward Seaga's conservative Jamaica Labour Party (JLP) in 1980 marked a move towards the restructuring of the banana industry, comparable in some respects to the experience of Dominica. Supported by the Reagan administration, the JLP government adopted a position of state disinvestment and called for the industry to be 'returned to the growers'. A USAID working paper of 1984 entitled 'The Banana Export Industry of Jamaica', recommended the reorganisation of the industry, reserving export production for a ▶

---

few large estates and relegating 'peasant' production to the supply of the domestic market. USAID also recommended the privatisation of shipping services — hitherto managed by the Jamaican Banana Company (BANCO) — and the selling of government-owned estates to the private sector.

As with Dominica, however, official proclamations of 'free market' policy are accompanied by considerable levels of continuing state involvement. A new organisation was founded in 1985 with the aim of stimulating banana production and handing it over to private enterprise. Known as the Banana Exporting Company (BECO), the body was intended to set the price for the fruit, organise shipping and, through the government marketing company operating in London (JAMCO), control the Jamaican banana market in the UK. The government claimed the right to name one member of the nine-strong board of the new company; the others would be growers' representatives.

Alongside this policy of state disengagement, however, stands the significant government involvement in the two largest recent development projects aimed at boosting export production of bananas. The first of these is the Eastern Banana Estates Ltd (EBEL) in St Thomas parish, containing 2,000 acres of pure stand land, in which the government owns 70 per cent of the equity, the Jamaica Banana Producers Association 20 per cent, and United Brands (Fyffes) 10 per cent. Four other projects include a further 11,000 acres of expanded or improved banana cultivation, all involving some form of government or international agency funding which requires a high government profile.

The restructuring of the Jamaican industry has yet to bring about the anticipated recovery in export figures. The expected total for 1987 is 35,000 tonnes, still well below the 150,000 tonnes which, according to Agriculture Ministry officials, are worth US$140 million as Jamaica's share of the guaranteed UK market. Moreover, the restructuring has forced several thousand marginally efficient farmers out of the industry, putting emphasis on high yields per acre. The closure of the Jamaica Banana Company, whose functions were turned over to the All-Island Banana Growers' Association, also cost an estimated 2,300 jobs in September 1985.

The Jamaican case reveals an industry forced to compete on the terms dictated by the banana multinationals and an aggressively pro-private sector government. Rather than help small farmers improve their cultivation or renegotiate the contract to ensure that savings go to the producer and not to the marketing firm or the UK consumer, the government encourages large-scale, capital-intensive estate production and, therefore, reduced employment in the industry. The motivation, inevitably, is profitability and improved returns for the large farmer and purchasing company. In a country with massive rural unemployment, this policy offers little hope to the poorest sectors of society.

overall consumption is larger than Grenada's export production and therefore represented a potential market of some importance. However, Colombia and Ecuador had a well-established trade with Eastern Europe and Grenada found it impossible to compete, even though an arrangement to export bananas to East Germany was planned.

The US invasion of October 1983 which brought down the PRG, ruled out any further independent search for new markets. Grenada, more than the other Windward Islands, has also been particularly hit by the deterioration in value of the UK pound in relation to the US dollar, to which the Eastern Caribbean dollar is tied. The closer ties with the US which followed the invasion meant that Grenada now imports an increasing share of its agricultural inputs from the US, for which payment must be made in US dollars. The result has been a corresponding drop in the island's national balance of payments and an increase in the cost of living for farmers, who effectively are paid in devalued pounds, but who must also buy imported food, farm inputs and consumer goods with US dollars.

The Grenadian banana industry entered a new crisis at the end of 1984. Early in 1985 WINBAN warned that shipments from Grenada would have to be suspended if the quality of the fruit did not improve. Investigating an alleged epidemic of leaf spot, a visiting WINBAN team was reportedly shocked by the state of Grenada's industry. Earnings dropped by 3.9 per cent to EC$7.9 million in 1984, and production fell to a new low of 8,857 tonnes. In the same year the Grenada Banana Cooperative Society announced a loss of EC$642,000.

With the closure of Grenada's four remaining boxing plants in August 1986, the island's banana industry was entirely restructured towards the field packing system. In the first half of that year banana production was reported to have increased slightly, but in September a major storm destroyed an estimated 60,000 plants, valued at EC$0.8 million.

Conclusion

The small banana farmers of the eastern Caribbean have little control over their futures and few options for improving their way of life. The structure of the international banana market favours the large corporations which control it. They secure high returns through their dominance over transportation, ripening and distribution. In the Windward Islands, all the risks and efforts of banana cultivation are borne by the farmers, who receive only a tiny portion of the final retail price of their crop.

The banana companies enjoy the flexibility which wealth and power give them. For instance, both Geest and the Caribbean farmer have had to face pressures from developments in the international banana market despite their protected access to the British market. But the ability to weather such pressure has been very different in each case.

Following the virtual collapse of Jamaican banana production in the early 1970s, Fyffes flooded the UK market with bananas from Central and South America. A subsidiary of the largest banana multinational, United Brands, Fyffes controlled 37 per cent of the UK's banana imports in 1981. United Brands has invested in capital intensive banana plantations for decades; yields and quality are superior to Caribbean production. In addition, much of this investment is amortised with sales to the large North American, European and Japanese markets, making the marginal cost of producing a few more tonnes for the smaller UK market quite low. Fyffes is therefore able to force Geest to compete on price.

The cost structure of Windward Island bananas is very different to their Latin American competitors. The rugged terrain of the islands does not lend itself to large capital investments which could reduce transport costs and improve yields significantly. Only the introduction of field packing offers some hope of improvement in the quality and volume of fruit exported. Geest claims that without the protection of UK import quotas, it is doubtful whether the Windward Island's lower quality and higher cost bananas would find a market at all.

Traditionally, Geest has been cushioned from the normal cost reductions associated with increased competition by the conditions of the banana export/import monopoly it enjoys. Its contracts with the growers' associations and WINBAN have tempered any incentive to modernise by allowing Geest to pass most cost increases onto the growers. The quotas imposed by the British government have permitted higher than international prices to prevail on the UK market. With only two firms supplying over 80 per cent of the UK banana market, Geest has been able to increase its profits beyond what competitive markets would allow. Over the years, together with the low prices paid to the Windward Island banana farmer, this situation has enabled Geest to grow from a modest bulb importer in the 1950s to a highly diversified conglomerate of 59 companies in the UK, Europe and the Caribbean; the largest UK importer of fruit and vegetables.

But despite the contribution of the Caribbean farmers to Geest's expansion, only 20 per cent of the company's sales currently comes from bananas. Geest now grows more flower bulbs in Lincolnshire than all of Holland, and in fact exports tulips to Holland! Diversification has enabled Geest to build some protection to the company from the vicissitudes of the international banana market.

The situation is very different for the Caribbean farmers. They remain dependent on one crop, at present 'in boom', but with no guarantee for the future. At the root of Geest's growth is the farmers' dependence on income from cash crops for the major part of their earnings. The Windwards import over 60 per cent of their food requirements and a greater percentage of other consumption goods. Cash is essential therefore, in order to buy many basic necessities. Historically deprived of sufficient land to grow enough food for their families, the West Indian peasantry has been forced to rely on multiple sources of income. These include wage labour on plantations, work in the tourist industry, remittances from family members who have emigrated, kitchen gardens and even landless farming (eg small livestock) as well as growing cash crops. But it is the latter which form the most regular source of cash income as earnings from wages and remittances are sporadic.

It is the regularity of banana income, not so much its size, which is crucial to the peasantry. No matter what the Green Market Price, farmers will sell bananas when the Geest boat arrives in order to maintain their consumption of basic goods.

This dependence on a regular income from bananas explains in large part the willingness of Windward farmers to continue selling bananas at what appears to be less than the cost of production. In fact, the cost of production quoted by those who claim the industry is losing money is imputed by the use of a hypothetical wage value for the farmers' labour which bears little relation to his or her actual income from bananas. Most farmers continue to sell bananas because they cannot afford to withhold their labour even if the actual 'wage' received is less than market labour rates. There are no real labour markets and no alternative means of making a living.

The shipment of bananas even at the height of the US invasion of Grenada shows the degree to which this dependency on banana income prevails. Geest's internal Second Annual Review noted:

> Despite the bloody coup in Grenada, followed by the intervention of the US forces, no bananas were left in the island. Although one of our ships had to wait a few days before collecting cargo, it was the first commercial ship in Grenada following the trouble. It was extremely welcome to the inhabitants and the Governor-General and other dignitaries took lunch on board whilst the bananas were loaded. It is hoped the island settles down quickly for we have been carrying all the high technology equipment from Plessey for the new airport being built.

It is not only the individual farmers who depend on Geest's regular purchase of bananas. Each island's balance of payments and tax revenues depend heavily on bananas. The governments of the islands tend to favour Geest in their negotiations rather than demand a better deal out of fear that the company will simply pull out. WINBAN has even been reluctant to ask for access to information about Geest's costs and is a somewhat toothless representative of the farmers' interests before the company.

Alternatives

Atherton Martin who was briefly Minister of Agriculture in Dominica in 1979, has remarked that Dominica is not really suited to the cultivation of bananas in competition with Central and South American plantations. He suggests that in the medium to long term, bananas should be phased out in favour of other vegetables, root crops and tree crops which are more suited to the particular agro-ecology and marketing capacity of Dominica.

Given the importance of a regular income from a guaranteed banana market to the majority of the Windward's small farmers, there is no quick and easy transition to alternative crops and markets. Efforts to resolve the region's agricultural problems will involve a complex process and several approaches. These might include:

● A long term strategy to improve the Windward farmers' share in banana exports to the protected UK market
● The development of new markets and other uses for bananas
● The diversification of agriculture towards food for local consumption and exports of crops which provide a better return to farmers.

Increasing revenue from banana production will be crucial to any planned transition to alternative crops. Much could be done to improve the quality and yields of existing production through better credit provision, giving the small farmer access to tools, fertiliser and other inputs. At present, most financial institutions including government programmes, base their lending decisions on the assumption that credit should be used for the purchase of more land, machinery and other capital inputs which can then be held as collateral in the event of default on a loan. Peasant farmers, however, invest labour rather than capital and their credit needs lie in labour saving hand tools, fertilisers and pesticides and occasionally, additional labour. These are not tangible or valuable assets for use as collateral but would nevertheless enable farmers to improve productivity and ultimately their ability to repay any loans.

Greater labour input into cultivation by the small farmer results in the effective devaluation of their 'wages' when prices are set by the international market. Small, inexpensive labour saving tools would greatly increase the returns to a small farmer's labour. The type of research needed to develop these tools is at present largely ignored by most governments and big corporations who are more interested in selling agricultural chemicals and large machinery rather than small, inexpensive hand tools.

Secondly, attempts could be made to capture a higher percentage of the retail price of bananas for the farmers. Such steps would, however, require a change in attitude on the part of WINBAN and ultimately, the respective island governments. They would need to take a tougher stance with Geest aimed at getting a better deal for the region's farmers.

There are four proposals for dealing with the loss of income resulting from exchange rate fluctuations:

1. The creation of an artificial 'banana pound' would involve a fixed exchange rate for the pound sterling, to be used to pay for banana exports. This proposal has been rejected by the British government.
2. The creation of a banana stabilisation fund to compensate farmers for losses of earnings arising from changes in the exchange rate.
3. To peg the EC dollar to an appropriate basket of currencies, in which changes with respect to one currency could be offset by movements in the others.
4. To peg the EC dollar to the pound officially.

The first two proposals would depend on the willingness of the British government, Geest and other governments to contribute to the fund; the others would require the eastern Caribbean countries to act together as a group.

The income of the small farmer could also be improved through the development of other uses for bananas and by-products. The Agency for Caribbean Transformation, based in Trinidad, has estimated that the development of a market for banana fibres could provide sufficient additional income per acre of land to enable the farmer to purchase the extra fertiliser and pesticides necessary to increase yields substantially. These fibres can be used for twine, paper, packaging material, fibreboard, woven products and crafts. An additional advantage would be the improvement of field hygiene through the removal of plant material which acts as a host for accumulated disease.

A study of the potential markets for banana fibre carried out in St Lucia by a consultant for a German aid agency, concluded that in principle, raw banana fibre could compete with sisal, jute, abaca and even synthetic fibres (though the latter was based on the assumption that petroleum costs would continue to rise which is not now the case). WINBAN could explore the possibility of producing boxes from banana fibre rather than importing paper pulp as at present.

Another advantage of such a scheme is its spin-off effect on local industry. At present the banana industry requires few local inputs which might stimulate domestic manufacturing. But the development of an industry based on banana fibres is technically and economically possible; it could occur on a small scale without the intervention of large corporations. A small fibre extraction industry has been set up in the Philippines, for example, which uses machinery developed and built by local blacksmiths.

The local design and construction of small factories using motors, pumps and assorted piping, wiring etc, is a very effective means of technology transfer. Although the individual components may have to be imported, they can be purchased on competitive international small machinery markets with a minimum of investment. Small-scale components can be combined in flexible designs which use technologies which are more appropriate for local raw material supplies than large or even medium-sized plants. The latter are often imported as turnkey or integrated projects using technologies developed for the particular raw material inputs of other countries. They are often designed on a much grander scale than what is normally required by the domestic markets of small third world nations.

Other potential by-products of the banana industry are vinegar, wines, flour and banana chips. Banana flour could be combined with wheat flour (from which the Windwards get some 30 per cent of their food energy and protein) to reduce imports of wheat significantly. Tests at the University of the West Indies have shown that up to 40 per cent banana flour can be used in these composite flours without seriously affecting either the texture or taste of bread and other flour products. Banana chips are a nutritious alternative to many 'junk foods' and snacks. When properly dried, they have a shelf life of up to six or more months, without using the many chemical additives used by the big convenience food manufacturers.

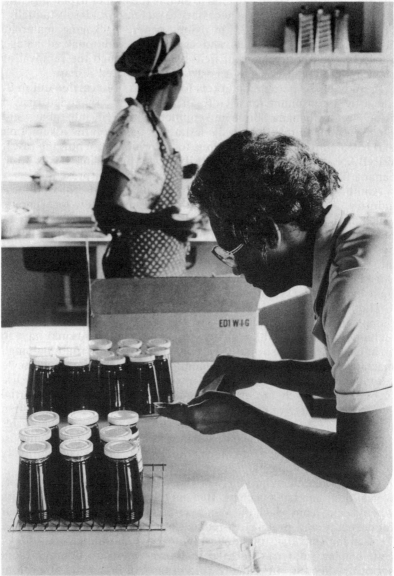

Food processing cooperative, St Vincent

Developments in biotechnology may open up new uses for bananas. The international food industry has been experimenting with food 'engineering' using a variety of raw material supplies. For instance, the list of contents on margarine packs in the supermarket suggests that the product may contain any of a number of oils, from soya, rapeseed, corn, coconut, cotton or others. The food multinationals are finding it difficult to decide which is the cheapest current source of raw material, but technically and economically it is possible to use a wide range of crops. This opens up markets for new third world commodities. Clive Thomas has studied the future of sucro-chemistry and its impact on the Caribbean sugar industry. He has pointed out that anything which can be synthesised from petroleum hydrocarbons can also theoretically be produced from sugar and many other commodity-based starches or carbohydrates. However, the six million tonnes of bananas exported annually would have to compete with 90 million tonnes of international sugar exports as well as other potential sources of carbohydrates. The commercial possibilities are evidently far fewer for bananas, which lessens the incentive for further research in banana starch chemistry.

There are considerable possibilities for alternative food crops in the Windward Islands. Geest has already recognised the potential by adding shipments of other crops to its regular banana consignment. The experience developed in the regional banana industry could easily be applied to other crops. There is now a relatively sophisticated organisation of packaging, transport and marketing of bananas. The agricultural supply data required for the marketing of alternative crops could be simply an extension of the elaborate system already installed to forecast banana plantings, fertiliser distribution, harvesting, boxing, transport and so on.

In Dominica the farmers themselves have taken the initiative to develop a Farm to Market Programme, which will sell their produce in Barbados, Trinidad, the French islands and even in more distant tourist resorts such as the Virgin Islands. This programme is about to acquire its own refrigerated vessel through the assistance of various international non-governmental aid agencies and has recently won a contract to supply large quantities of grapefruit to McCains, a big Canadian food processing company.

There are, therefore, a range of options which could be explored as a means of increasing income and reducing dependency in the Windward Islands. Political will is, however, a prerequisite for pursuing such options. While the small farmers remain a weak and unorganised force it is unlikely that the region's governments would consider doing so. The islands' politicians have mostly grown accustomed to a relation of dependency, first with the UK, more recently with the US. The pursuit of aid packages through appropriate political alliances, foreign investment through generous tax benefits, and foreign exchange through the 'tourist plantation', is preferred by the islands' elites to a strategy of self-reliance and balanced development.

Grenada's attempt to pursue an alternative path of development under the New Jewel Movement, has now been widely discredited. During the NJM government, the US did its utmost to undermine its programme and isolate it from its Caribbean neighbours. The US invasion stands today as a warning to all who wander outside its sphere of influence. Although the internal conflicts within the NJM provided the US with an excuse to invade, since then it has used every possible opportunity to discredit everything associated with the Grenadian revolution, including some of its very successful social and economic programmes.

Until new alternatives emerge, the lives of the small farmers will remain very much as we have described. As Atherton Martin writes:

> Sadly, the one significant agricultural industry keeping the farmer going economically is bananas, an industry where pricing, marketing and transport are controlled by a foreign corporation; an industry which is dependent on preferential tariff protection by a foreign government; a crop which is prone to devastation by annual hurricanes, and in which the farmer has a decreasing say in matters affecting the industry's future.

Bibliography

ACP/EEC, *The Banana Trade and the ACP States.* Issue no 78, pp 64-91, Brussels, March-April 1983.

Ambursley F, and Cohen R, (eds), *Crisis in the Caribbean.* London, Heinemann, 1983.

Barry, T, Wood, B, and Preusch, D, *Dollars and Dictators: A Guide to Central America.* The Resource Center, Albuquerque, 1982.

Barry, T, Wood, B, and Preusch, D, *The Other Side of Paradise: Foreign Control in the Caribbean.* The Resource Center, Albuquerque, 1984.

Bourne, C, 'Small Farming in Dominica', in *Small Farming in the Less Developed Countries of the Commonwealth Caribbean.* Caribbean Development Bank, Barbados, 1980.

Brizan, G, *Grenada: Island of Conflict.* London, Zed Books, 1984.

Burgaud, Jean-Marie, *The New Caribbean Deal: The Next Five Years.* Economist Intelligence Unit, London, 1986.

Cargill, Morris, 'Why the Decline in the Banana Industry?' *Jamaica Daily Gleaner.* Kingston, 21 January 1985.

Caribbean Centre for Action Research (CCAR), *Action Oriented Research into the Production and Marketing of Bananas in Dominica: A Preliminary Investigation.* mimeo, July 1978.

CIDA, *Country Programme Review: Leeward and Windward Islands.* Canadian International Development Agency, Ottawa, 10 February, 1983.

Clairmont Fredrick, *The Banana Empire.* CERES, Rome, Jan/Feb 1975, pp 31-34.

CLAT-Nederland, *Handel en wandel van het multinationale bedrijf Geest.* Utrecht, 1975.

Coke, L B and Gomes, P I, *Agriculture.* Caribbean Technology Policy Studies Project, University of the West Indies and University of Guyana, mimeo, St Augustine, Trinidad.

Cole, Joyce, *The Socio-Cultural Factors Involved in Production by Small Farmers in St Lucia of Bananas and Tomatoes and their Marketing.* UNESCO, Rome, 1980.

Commonwealth Secretariat, *The Export Marketing Arrangements of the Windward Islands Banana Industry.* Economic Affairs Division, Commonwealth Secretariat, mimeo, London, March 1981.

Dominica Farmers Union, *Bananas and the Dominican Economy: What is to be done?* mimeo, Roseau, Dominica, November 1982.

Economist, The, *The Formation of European Banana Prices: An Analysis of the Market Forces Involved.* Economist Intelligence Unit Special Report, London, October 1980.

Ellis, F, *An Institutional Approach to Tropical Commodity Trade: Case Study of Banana Exports from the Commonwealth Caribbean*. Report for the Commonwealth Secretariat, mimeo, May 1975.

Ellis F, *Las Transnacionales del banano en Centroamerica*. Educa, San José, Costa Rica, 1983.

FAO, *The World Banana Economy 1970-1984*. FAO Economic and Social Development Paper 57, Rome, 1986.

Fruit Trades Journal, *The UK Banana Industry*, banana supplement, 26 April 1985.

Geest Industries, *Report and Accounts*, 1980-1986.

Government of St Lucia, *Inquiry into the Banana Industry*. Final Report, Castries, 1980.

Government of St Lucia, *Land Reform Commission*. Final Report, Castries, November 1981.

Hart, Herber and Black, Clinton, *Jamaica's Banana Industry: A History of the Banana Industry with Particular Reference to the Part Played by the Jamaica Banana Producers Association Ltd*. JBPA, Kingston, Jamaica, 1984.

Henderson, T H and Gomes, P I, *A Profile of Small Farming in St Vincent, Dominica and St Lucia: Report of a Baseline Survey*. St Augustine, Trinidad, University of the West Indies, Agricultural Extension Depts, 1979.

Krehm, William, *Democracies and Tyrannies of the Caribbean*. Connecticut, Lawrence Hill and Company, 1984.

Labour Research Department, *Geest Holdings Ltd*. Labour Research Department, Company Information Service, London, November 1978.

Lewis, Gordon K, *The Growth of the Modern West Indies*. London, Macgibbon and Kee, 1968.

LeFranc, E R, 'Small Farming in Grenada, St Vincent and St Lucia', in *Small Farming in the Less Developed Countries of the Commonwealth Caribbean*. Caribbean Development Bank, Barbados, 1980.

Marie, J M, *Agricultural Diversification in a Small Economy: The Case for Dominica*. ISER Occasional Paper, no 10, University of the West Indies, Jamaica, 1979.

McLindon, M, *The Banana Export Industry of Jamaica*. USAID Working Paper, Kingston, Jamaica, September 1984.

Mourillon, V J F, *The Dominica Banana Industry from Inception to Independence, 1928-78*. Dominica Banana Growers Association, Roseau, Dominica, 1979.

Read, Robert, 'The Growth and Structure of Multinationals in the Banana Export Trade', *The Growth of International Business*. George, Allen and Unwin, London, 1983.

Resource Center, *Focus on the Eastern Caribbean: Bananas, Bucks and Boots*, The Resource Center, Albuquerque, 1984.

Rural Transformation Collective, *Bananas and Poverty*. mimeo Castries, St Lucia, 1978.

Thomas, Clive Y, *Sugar: An Assessment of the Impact of Technological Development in the High Fructose Corn Syrup and Sucrochemicals*.

International Development Research Centre, Ottawa, 1985.

Thomson, R, *The Potential and Limits of Agricultural Self-Reliance in Grenada*. Unpublished MA thesis, School of International Affairs, Carleton University, Ottawa, 1983.

UK Price Commission, *Prices on Distribution of Bananas*. Report no 4, HMSO, London, 1974.

West Indies Royal Commission Report (The Moyne Commission). HMSO, London, 1945.

Williams, E, *From Columbus to Castro: The History of the Caribbean 1492-1969*. Andre Deutsch, London, 1970.

World Bank, *St Lucia: Economic Performance and Prospects*. 1985.

Whose Gold?

Geest and the Banana Trade

Half the bananas eaten in Britain are grown on the islands of the Eastern Caribbean and one British-based company, Geest, imports them all.

Whose Gold? is a new learning resource for secondary schools on Geest and the Eastern Caribbean banana industry. It looks at:

The banana trade: Growing, pricing and profits — who gets what?

Work: Banana work in Britain and the Caribbean — conditions, workers' organisations and relations with Geest.

Geest — the multinational: The company and its operations at the local, national and international level.

Development: A brief history of British involvement and banana growing in Dominica, Grenada, St Lucia and St Vincent.

Future prospects: A role play looking at the banana industry and alternatives to the present structure, as seen from the point of view of different groups involved — growers, union officials, Geest managers, packers and retailers in Britain.

Whose Gold? — a large format booklet with photos, cartoons, interviews and other illustrations. Participatory activities for mixed ability groups explore common themes for communities in Britain and the Caribbean. Relevant for development education, social studies, geography, modern studies and anti-racist education.

Available Autumn 1987   Price £1.95
from Latin America Bureau
1 Amwell Street, London EC1R 1UL   ISBN 0 906156 28 9

Other LAB titles on the Caribbean

'well researched and easy to read publications'
Caribbean Contact, Barbados

The Poor and the Powerless: Economic Policy and Change in the Caribbean
by Clive Y. Thomas

A major new study by Guyanese development economist, C.Y. Thomas. This book offers an introduction to the Caribbean for non-specialists and a powerful critique of the 'development strategies' pursued in the region over the past decades.
Published January 1988

Under the Eagle: US Intervention in Central America and the Caribbean
by Jenny Pearce
Updated edition April 1982. 295pp. £5.95

Guyana: Fraudulent Revolution
March 1984. 106pp. £3.50

'For Guyanese and anyone else wishing to understand contemporary Guyana, *Fraudulent Revolution* represents the missing link'
West Indian World.

Grenada: Whose Freedom?
by Fitzroy Ambursley and James Dunkerley.
April 1984. 128pp. £3.50

'A valuable contribution to the debate on Grenada and well worth reading'
Caribbean Times

Haiti: Family Business
by Rod Prince
September 1985. 86pp. £3.50

' . . . not only a complete reference source on Haiti, but a lucid, hard-hitting and tragic story of this impoverished and inflexible country'
Caribbean Insight

Prices do not include postage

Latin America Bureau

The Latin America Bureau is a small, independent, non-profit making research organisation established in 1977. LAB is concerned with human rights and related social, political and economic issues in Central and South America and the Caribbean. We carry out research and publish books, publicise and lobby on these issues and establish support links with Latin American groups. We also brief the media, organise seminars and have a growing programme of schools publications.

WOW Campaigns Limited is a non-profit making, distributing, limited company which campaigns against the causes of poverty and provides general support for the charity War on Want; War on Want funds practical development projects which aim to eradicate poverty in 30 countries of Asia, Africa and Latin America.